Taking Your Kindle Fire
to the Max

Mark Rollins
thegeekchurch.com

Apress®

Taking Your Kindle Fire to the Max

ISBN-13 (pbk): 978-1-4302-4263-5

ISBN-13 (electronic): 978-1-4302-4264-2

Trademarked names, logos, and images may appear in this book. Rather than use a trademark symbol with every occurrence of a trademarked name, logo, or image we use the names, logos, and images only in an editorial fashion and to the benefit of the trademark owner, with no intention of infringement of the trademark.

The use in this publication of trade names, trademarks, service marks, and similar terms, even if they are not identified as such, is not to be taken as an expression of opinion as to whether or not they are subject to proprietary rights.

President and Publisher: Paul Manning
Lead Editor: Michelle Lowman
Development Editor: Douglas Pundick
Technical Reviewer: Marziah Karch
Editorial Board: Steve Anglin, Ewan Buckingham, Gary Cornell, Louise Corrigan, Morgan Ertel, Jonathan Gennick, Jonathan Hassell, Robert Hutchinson, Michelle Lowman, James Markham, Matthew Moodie, Jeff Olson, Jeffrey Pepper, Douglas Pundick, Ben Renow-Clarke, Dominic Shakeshaft, Gwenan Spearing, Matt Wade, Tom Welsh
Coordinating Editor: Jessica Belanger
Copy Editor: Kimberly Burton
Compositor: MacPS, LLC
Indexer: SPi Global
Artist: SPi Golbal
Cover Designer: Anna Ishchenko

Distributed to the book trade worldwide by Springer Science+Business Media, LLC., 233 Spring Street, 6th Floor, New York, NY 10013. Phone 1-800-SPRINGER, fax (201) 348-4505, e-mail orders-ny@springer-sbm.com, or visit www.springeronline.com.

For information on translations, please e-mail rights@apress.com, or visit www.apress.com.

Apress and friends of ED books may be purchased in bulk for academic, corporate, or promotional use. eBook versions and licenses are also available for most titles. For more information, reference our Special Bulk Sales–eBook Licensing web page at www.apress.com/bulk-sales.

The information in this book is distributed on an "as is" basis, without warranty. Although every precaution has been taken in the preparation of this work, neither the author(s) nor Apress shall have any liability to any person or entity with respect to any loss or damage caused or alleged to be caused directly or indirectly by the information contained in this work.

Contents at a Glance

Contents

About the Author

Mark Rollins was born in Seattle in 1971. He attended Washington State University in Pullman, Washington, graduating in 1994 with a degree in English. After college, he began to write skits for college-age groups.

After four years working for Wal-Mart, and another five years working for Schweitzer Engineering Laboratories (SEL), he decided to pursue a full-time career in writing beginning in 2005.

Since then, he has written for many tech and gadget blogs, including screenhead.com, image-acquire.com, cybertheater.com, mobilewhack.com, carbuyersnotebook.com, gearlive.com, zmogo.com, gadgetell.com, gadgets-weblog.com, androidedge.com, and coolest-gadgets.com. He has also written for video game blogs such as gamertell.com and digitalbattle.com.

In 2009, Mark decided to write his own tech and gadget blog, known as The Geek Church (www.TheGeekChurch.com). The purpose of the blog is to report on the latest in technology, as well as inform the church-going crowd (who are often not very technically adept) on the benefits of using more technology in the ministry. Since 2012, Mark has completely devoted his time to this blog, and considers it his ministry and mission.

Mark currently resides in Pullman, Washington, with his wife and three children.

About the Technical Reviewer

Marziah Karch enjoys the challenge of explaining complex technology to beginning audiences. She is an education technologist for Johnson County Community College in the Kansas City metro area with over ten years of experience. She holds an MS in instructional design and has occasionally taught credit courses in interactive media.

Marziah also contributes to *New York Times*-owned About.com and has been their "Guide to Google" since 2006. She's written several books for Apress, including *Android Tablets Made Simple* (2011). When she's not feeding her geek-side with new gadgets or writing about technology, Marziah enjoys life in Lawrence, Kansas, with her husband, Harold, and two children.

Acknowledgments

Normally, this is a place where you acknowledge people who helped you along the way. Don't worry, I will get to that, but I want to bring up something that I can't help but acknowledge.

While I was writing this book, I took a road trip in early January of 2012. I wanted my family to visit my wife's mother and sister in Pocatello, Idaho. After a week in Pocatello, I drove solo to Las Vegas for the Consumer Electronics Show (CES). When the big technological expo was over, I returned to Pocatello and picked up my family to drive back to Pullman.

On January 15, 2012, my family and I were in a terrible automobile accident.

What you are seeing here in this photo is my car, or what was left of it. What happened was one of my tires blew out, and when I tried to pull over, the car rolled. I'm not certain what happened after that, because I suffered a head injury.

I woke up in the hospital two days later, and I was relieved to know that my wife and kids were still alive. It is a miracle that we all lived, and I was also amazed that my Kindle Fire and my laptop came through without a scratch. I guess stuffing my laptop bag underneath the backseat kept it from tumbling with the rest of our stuff.

I found that after this accident, a lot of people came to help our family. One of them was my wife's mother, Karen Collins, who took care of our kids for a few days while my wife and I were in the hospital. I also want to thank Wayne Wheylan, who gave us a ride home after our car was irreparably damaged.

I also want to thank all the people who prayed for my family as we went through this time. So many people have helped us out, like Katheren Gomez, who gave us rides when we didn't have a car of our own.

I also want to thank Ann Parks, my insurance agent at State Farm who helped our family out immensely. She is like a good neighbor.

This incident has taught me how important life is, as my family and I were very fortunate to survive this accident. After I got back home, it took a while to get back to a normal life. Editing the last part of this book after the accident really helped me feel like I was living again, after the accident left me with some side effects. Despite the negative consequences, I am very glad for this experience overall.

I would also like to give special acknowledgement to the following people:

Michelle Lowman, Kelly Moritz, and Jessica Belanger as well as other editors at Apress who helped me with this book. I really appreciate your understanding after the accident, and I had a lot of help after the book was nearing completion.

Kristina Rollins, my beautiful wife and the mother of my three wonderful children. I don't know what I would do without you.

Al Carlton, who gave me a terrific opportunity for writing for coolest-gadgets.com for many years.

Pastors Phil and Kari Vance, who worked behind the scenes after the accident to make certain we came home.

—Mark Rollins

Introduction

The Digital Age

With the advent of the internet , the proliferation of mobile phones, and the rapid development of wireless technologies, we are truly living in a digital age.

It seems like only yesterday that we were using dial-up, and that awful scream from the modem meant that we were online at data speeds that would seem like a snail's pace compared to today. Not only has our internet improved, but the way our telephone system has changed in the past decade has been nothing short of dynamic. Some of us can still remember a time when calling someone meant he or she had to be at home in order to answer the phone. Considering that most people carry around their phones with them, we almost don't have an excuse for returning our phone calls.

It's funny how quickly this technology has changed in such a short time. These days, I wonder how I lived before without fast internet and mobile phones, and now I am getting impatient for new tech to come out, just so I can do my work even faster.

There are many reasons why this digital age is progressing so quickly. Perhaps we realized that we could save several tree forests by putting documents on digital files. Maybe it is just easier to retrieve files with the click of a mouse, rather than taking them out of a filing cabinet. Whatever the case, the use of paper is in decline, and the need for digital memory is continually on the rise.

I'm sure that most of you have realized that there isn't any need for a paper bill to be sent to your house when an e-mail or text message can simply alert you to the amount that you owe. Then, instead of writing a check, sticking it into and envelope, and sending it on its way, you can simply go to your online bank account and pay that bill electronically. Gone are the days when you had to sit at your desk and work out the bills with paper, checks, and pen—because you can now pay them electronically.

The Age of E-books

Books can be made digital, too. Why should we go through the costly and often environmentally unfriendly process just to get paper, and then run it all through a printing press? Isn't it just easier and faster to type up all the words on a word-processing program, and then put them in a digital format?

Amazon.com combined both the digital world with the traditional book format when they got into the online retailing business back in 1995. Their slogan was "The World's Biggest Bookstore," and the company became the world's biggest in online retailing. Even after the dot-com boom, the company still had enormous success. Amazon CEO Jeff Bezos was named *Time* Magazine's Man of the Year in 1999.

In 2007, Amazon.com took another giant step in e-books when Bezos unveiled the Kindle. The company realized that people want to read classic and contemporary books, and that they were willing to sacrifice traditional book formats for the convenience of a mobile device. In short, the Kindle e-book reader met a realization that people needed to be less dependent on paper and take advantage of the digital formats already in use on their computers.

Thanks to this e-reader technology, thousands of books can be downloaded to a single device the size of a tablet, often at a cheaper price. Amazon may not have been the first to get an e-reader out to the market, but they definitely made themselves to be the most popular of the device type.

Are We Ever Going to Get Away from Traditional Books?

Are we looking at an age when traditional books are going to be left behind? Even though e-book sales are good, traditional book sales are still going strong. I suppose that old habits die hard, and I can honestly say that reading books on an e-reader is a different experience than traditional page-turning.

However, the difference is slight. When it really comes down to it, isn't it the words on a page that people really want? Does it really make a difference if it is on a paper page or a digital screen? Amazon recently made fun of this in a series of commercials simply called "Friends."

Figure 1. *A still shot from a series of Amazon.com commercials called "Friends." In the commercials, the woman is a traditional book reader and the man owns a Kindle. You can probably guess the direction the commercial takes on which is the better choice.*

In the first of these commercials, the woman in the ad claims that traditional books are better because one can have "the satisfaction of folding down a page." Yes, that is completely ridiculous, and it is planned that way. The second in the series of commercials discusses how the Kindle can access a book within a minute, thereby negating a trip to the bookstore. The third and last of this series shows the woman talking about how her new bag can hold some reading material, but the Kindle can hold a lot more.

Yes, the benefits of e-books compared to traditional paper books are obvious, and it would appear that Amazon is ready for an era where electronic books would be the norm for book reading. Considering that most books are using paper that will eventually turn to dust after a few decades, even the newest books we have now don't have too long of a lifespan. It doesn't look like traditional books have been completely "phased out" as yet, and it would probably take many years before that would happen. Then again, if we can get a generation raised comfortably on e-books, I would imagine that it wouldn't be too difficult for the next generation to read nothing but e-books.

There seems to be some recent evidence to support this complete shift from books to e-books. In July of 2010, Bezos announced that, "the Kindle format has now overtaken the hardcover format." It was beginning to sell 80 percent more downloaded books than hardbacks. In May of the following year, Amazon stated that it sells 105 electronic books for every 100 printed ones.

In March 2011, before Andy Rooney left *60 Minutes*, he discussed how there are more e-books sold than actual paperback books. He said that he "doubted that," but according to Amazon, this is quite true. As you might have guessed, Rooney is one of those who will probably never embrace the e-book format.

It would appear that paper books are being phased out, but this is not something that is going to happen quickly. Some will probably never accept e-books no matter how easy they are to obtain. I know that my mother will not quit her traditional way of paying bills, even though I have tried to show her the ease of electronic bill paying. Since there are die-hards who will demand paper printed books, there will always be a place for traditional hardback and paperback books.

As future generations become adjusted to e-books, then we might be looking a future full of e-readers. Most smartphone owners have some sort of e-reader application, but the small screen on smartphones can make it harder to read. Tablet computers could be a substitute, but they are often too expensive for many consumers. E-readers, with their lower prices, have been a low-priced alternative for many years.

How Will the Kindle Fire Change the World?

The Kindle Fire is instrumental in today's digital market because it is an affordable tablet computer that promises to give users exactly what they want: content. This is one of the reasons why the Amazon has had amazing success— they give content to their users wherever and whenever in whatever form, be it print, video, or audio. Amazon has partnered with hundreds of magazines and newspapers to make certain they can deliver much content to their users, and there will be more formats to be delivered for the future.

Another reason the Kindle Fire will change the world is that it will allow more authors a wider platform for self publishing. Amazon intends self-published authors to keep 70 percent of the profits, and even big-name authors might want to go this route instead of with traditional publishers.

In addition to this, users have full access to Android, an open-source operating system that is already extremely popular on smartphones and tablets. As someone who loves the Android operating system, I am looking forward to seeing more Android users with a new crop of Kindle Fire users.

By the way, if you are looking for a way to market Android applications, feel free to pick up my book *The Business of Android Apps Development: Making and Marketing Apps that Succeed* (Apress, 2011). But enough talk about my former book, this book is about how you can make the most out of your Kindle Fire. So let's talk about how this book is organized.

- Chapter 1 discusses what to do with the Kindle Fire when it is out of the box, which includes charging and setting up the Kindle Fire to work with your Amazon.com account.

- Chapter 2 covers the basics of the Android operating system on the Kindle Fire. The Kindle Fire is an Android tablet, and this chapter will tell you the basics of interfacing with the Kindle Fire, including the Quick Settings.

▒ Chapter 3 talks about a Kindle Fire maintenance plan. Like any mobile device, it is often a discipline to use it daily, and some accessories are needed. This chapter discusses the habits and accessories you will want to have for the Kindle Fire.

▒ Chapter 4 details the Newsstand. The Kindle Fire is excellent for reading e-journals like magazines and newspapers. This chapter shows how to read, purchase, and subscribe to these e-journals, as well as how to get some magazine apps.

▒ In Chapter 5, I cover reading books on the Kindle Fire. Like earlier versions of the Kindle, the Fire is terrific for reading. Not only are traditional books available here, but there are many children's and comic books ready to buy.

▒ Chapter 6 is about music. For those that want to use the Kindle Fire for tunes, you can purchase tunes on the Amazon music store. You can also transfer tunes from a CD and iTunes for even more music options.

▒ Watching video on the Kindle Fire is an extra bonus, and you can rent or buy movies and television shows from Amazon's video store. Amazon Prime can provide even more options. This is all covered in Chapter 7.

▒ In addition to the books, magazines, music, and video, you can load your own digital content onto the Kindle wirelessly or wired thanks to the Docs category. Find out how to do that in Chapter 8.

▒ Since the Kindle Fire is an Android tablet, it is capable of supporting apps. Chapter 9 is where you learn how to download them, organize them, and delete them.

▒ Chapter 10 discusses using the web. Yes, the Kindle Fire can surf the web thanks to the Silk browser, and this chapter shows how to work it, as well as the bookmarks and settings.

▒ As long as you have the Kindle Fire wirelessly synced on a hot spot, you have access to e-mail. You can use e-mail from the web browser, or you can use the included e-mail app on many accounts. Chapter 11 discusses how to use them.

▒ Chapter 12 covers social networking. If you are into Facebook, Twitter, LinkedIn, Google + or any other social network on your computer, then you will be overjoyed that you can do these social networks on the Kindle Fire. In fact, there are apps so you can manage many social networks at once, and you can learn about them here.

▒ Chapter 13 details Quickoffice and Quickoffice Pro. Considering that the Kindle Fire comes with Quickoffice as a default program, then you should learn how to use this word processing program that works with Word, Excel, PowerPoint, and Adobe PDF documents.

▒ In Chapter 14, I discuss various, miscellaneous applications that will make your Kindle more fun and enable you to be more productive.

So, You Just Purchased an Amazon Kindle Fire. Now What?

Webster's Dictionary defines the word "Kindle" as to start, cause, or begin burning. I suppose that the obvious upgrade of a device called a Kindle would be Fire. For years, Amazon has dominated the e-book industry, and the Amazon Kindle Fire tablet is quite a leap into a new type of market. Not only did Amazon make a top-of-the-line tablet, but they are selling it at an MSRP (manufacturer's suggested retail price) of $199. By offering a tablet computer at a low price, Amazon is giving its customers the best of both worlds. A report from iSuppli, a leading market research firm, stated that the Kindle Fire actually costs $201.70 to make, which means that Amazon loses an estimated $2.70 for every Kindle Fire sold.

How can Amazon afford such a loss? The answer is one word: content. Amazon knows that if you are buying a Kindle Fire, then you are going to want the latest in magazines, books, video, music, and apps. You are going to pay for this service—and it is amazing how the small prices you pay for songs, e-books, videos, e-magazines, and Android apps can add up. I believe that Amazon's business plan is to offset the cost of the low-priced Kindle Fire with the monies that Kindle Fire consumers will spend on content, making it a possible "loss leader." So, it isn't too great a risk on Amazon's part.

If there is one fact that remains solid in the information age, it is that content is king. Amazon owes its success to the presentation of content, whether it be printed books, e-books, or any other type of media. The Kindle Fire empowers the customer to find the content that they want, in whatever form, for a small price that can and probably will easily add up to a big one.

Content is the main reason why consumers purchased the Kindle Fire. I'm sure that if I asked every Kindle Fire user why he or she made this purchase, I would get a great variety of answers. If I were to graph all the answers on a pie chart, the following would form the biggest of slices:

- I want a device that lets me read e-books.

- I want to forget about print magazines and newspapers. From now on, I want to use the Kindle Fire to read electronic journals.

- I want to keep my data on a cloud platform.

- I want to take advantage of the Android operating system on the Kindle Fire.

Whatever the reason for your purchase, I want to let you know how you can get books, magazines, newspapers, music, video, Android apps, or whatever else you desire on your Kindle Fire. Apress has published many "… to the Max" books, and like others in the series, the goal of this particular book is to make certain that you are using your device to its full potential!

Before I get into a discussion on the Kindle Fire, I want to briefly touch on the success of Amazon's famous e-reader.

History of the Amazon Kindle

Amazon changed the e-book reader market with the Kindle. The company is taking it a step further with the Kindle Fire. Right now, you may be holding this book in one hand while you have the Kindle Fire in the other. Better yet, perhaps you are even reading this book on the Kindle Fire or one of the earlier versions of the Kindle. In looking at the history of Kindle, you will see an evolution of Amazon's famous e-book reader device.

Kindle (Original Version)

The original Kindle launched in 2007; it was a push by Amazon to dominate the e-reader market. In short, it worked: it sold out in about five and a half hours, and remained out of stock for six months. At the time, the Kindle had 250 MB of memory, but it was the only model that was expandable with an SD card slot. It was sufficient enough to hold 200 non-illustrated titles viewable on a six-inch, four-level, gray scale display.

The introduction of the Kindle spawned a whole slough of imitator e-book readers. Most of them had similar features.

One of the more notable competitors is the Barnes & Noble NOOK, an e-book reader based on the Android platform. Its first version was released in 2009 at the price of $259. The price kept shrinking due to lack of demand and the release of the NOOK Wi-Fi and Simple Touch Reader. The NOOK Color was released in November of 2010 at a cost of $249 and came with Android 2.1, a seven-inch screen, and a microSD expansion slot. The NOOK Tablet came out one year later at the same price point, with 16 GB of internal storage and a microSDHC slot for up to 32 GB of memory.

Kindle 2

There weren't too many changes with the Kindle 2. It launched in February 2009 with an improved keyboard design. (The original Kindle keyboard had the characters on strange diagonals, which users either loved or hated.) The Kindle 2 also had a rough text-to-speech option, as well as a slimmer design.

In October of 2009, Amazon announced the international version of the Kindle 2. It had a mobile network standard that allowed it to download new titles in over 100 countries.

Kindle DX

The Kindle DX was announced in May 2009. It expanded the screen to 9.7 inches and it was supposed to support larger formats like magazines, newspapers, and textbooks. But the launch of the iPad and other tablet PCs eclipsed its sales. Like the Kindle 2, it followed-up with an international version.

It also had a version called the Kindle DX Graphite, which was known for its E Ink display with a 50 percent contrast ratio. It was named for its graphite-colored case. Many referred to the DX Graphite as "third generation," but this actually came later.

Kindle 3 or Kindle Keyboard

When the Kindle 3 came out, Amazon referred to it as the "Kindle Keyboard." (Amazon does not prefer a numbering system based on the generation of Kindle.) The Kindle Keyboard had a very small price point of $139, and had Wi-Fi-only and 3G versions.

It was followed by a slightly cheaper Kindle with special offers. Shortly after it hit the market, in December 2010, Amazon declared the third-generation Kindle as the bestselling product in the company's history.

Four New Members of the Kindle Family

In October 2011, Amazon announced that it was bringing four new members to the Kindle family. Three of them were similar to past Kindle models, but the fourth would be completely different.

Newest Generation of Kindle

One of the new versions is the Kindle 4 (again, not an official name). This version is 30 percent lighter (at 5.98 ounces), 18 percent smaller, and turns pages 10 percent faster than the previous version. It has a six-inch, E Ink display and is small enough to fit in a pocket.

The Kindle Touch

The Kindle Touch was released at about the same time as the Kindle 4. As implied by its name, this version has an easy-to-use touchscreen that makes it simple to turn pages, search, shop, and take notes on what Amazon calls "the most advanced electronic ink display." Another terrific feature of the Kindle Touch is the X-Ray, which enables customers to "explore the bones" of a book. Users can tap a control that will bring up more information on a book, including the ideas, characters, figures, and places or topics that interest them. This feature allows Kindle users to have more knowledge about the content of their reading material.

The Kindle Touch 3G

The Amazon Kindle Touch 3G is what the company calls a "top-of-the-line e-reader." Like the Kindle Touch, it is small and light with an easy-to-use touchscreen. As the name implies, it has 3G so the user doesn't have to continually search for a Wi-Fi hot spot, giving the reader the ability to download and read books at any time, anywhere, in over 100 countries around the world. Best of all, Amazon pays for the 3G connection and has no monthly fee or annual contract.

The New Class of Kindle

In its official press release of the Kindle Fire tablet, Amazon called it "a new class of Kindle." Considering that the device is not exclusively an e-reader, it is a fitting description. As of this writing, the Kindle Fire is the dominant species on the Kindle evolutionary scale.

Features of the Kindle Fire

This book devotes entire chapters on the features of the Kindle Fire. You will discover a lot of features that set it apart from earlier versions of the Kindle, including the following:

- A seven-inch color touchscreen with 16 million colors in high resolution, at 169 pixels per inch.

- A 1 GHz dual-core processor that provides the ability to browse the web or read books while downloading videos.

- About 8 GB of memory.

- Amazon Silk, a new cloud-accelerated web browser that uses "split browser" architecture using Amazon Web Services. A user's web page requests are sent through a service in the Amazon Elastic Compute Cloud (EC2) for processing. The service acts as a caching service, as well as a staging area where the complete bits of web pages can be pre-processed before being redirected to the user's browser.

- Free storage of all Amazon digital content in the Amazon Cloud.

- Amazon Whispersync, which allows Amazon to automatically sync your content with information like the last page read, bookmarks, and notes across a wide range of devices and platforms.

- One free month of Amazon Prime, which provides unlimited, commercial-free, instant streaming of over 11,000 movies and television shows; it includes Prime Instant Videos as well as free, two-day shipping on millions of items from Amazon.

- Over 100,000 television shows and movies from Amazon Instant Video, including new releases of popular TV shows.

- Over 17,000 songs from Amazon MP3, which includes new and bestselling albums.

- Over 100 exclusive graphic novels, some never before available in electronic format.

- Access to hundreds of magazines and newspapers, including some of the most popular, with full-color layouts, photographs, and illustrations, as well as built-in video, audio, and other interactive features.

- For the first time, the Kindle is powered by the Android operating system (OS). The version of Android is a customized version of Gingerbread (version 2.3).

Purchasing the Kindle Fire

Just as experts recommend buying an iDevice at an Apple store, buyers should purchase the Kindle Fire directly from Amazon. Considering that Amazon made its mark by selling materials online, most people, including you, probably purchased their Kindle Fire online. As mentioned, the Kindle is Amazon's greatest-selling product in the company history, but I would not be surprised if the Kindle Fire beats this record. Amazon's 2011 fourth-quarter earnings showed that it sold about 3.9 million Kindle Fire units, a number that could easily rise during the following year.

Some of you might have read *Taking Your iPad to the Max* by Michael Grothaus and Steve Sande (Apress, 2010) and discovered that some iPads have problems such as dead screen pixels. A lot of mobile electronics have problems that are discovered shortly after purchase. I'm sure that most of you can share a story about how your mobile phone had problems and how you had to use the insurance program that you purchased from your carrier in order to resolve it.

In the same way, you will want to make certain that you have all the purchase information about your Kindle Fire readily available should any problems arise. Your Kindle Fire comes with a brown card that details how to start it. On that back of the card are terms and policies, and how the Kindle Fire is covered by a one-year warranty. Like all high-priced electronics purchases, you will want to save your box in case you have to put everything back in its original packaging and send your Kindle Fire back to Amazon.

SquareTrade, an independent warranty provider, offers a Kindle Fire warranty that costs $44.99 for two years and includes accident protection. You can read more about it at www.amazon.com/SquareTrade-Warranty-Accident-Protection-customers/dp/B0058WELD2. It is up to you to decide if this is a good deal for you.

Figure 1-1. *My Kindle Fire when it arrived, oblong box and all*

Unboxing Your Kindle Fire

When you open up the packaging for your Kindle Fire, you find the unit, a charging cord, and a brown card that tells you what to do with it, as shown in Figure 1–2.

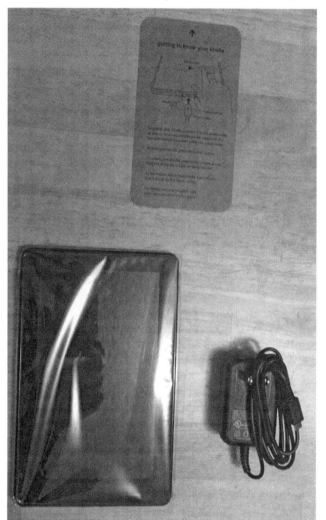

Figure 1–2. *There is only the unit itself, a charging cord, and a card that tells you what to do. That is all.*

As you can see in Figure 1–3, Amazon's Kindle Fire has very little as far as external controls.

Figure 1–3. *The Kindle Fire ports and controls*

On the side of the Kindle Fire you will find its ports. There is only one button; it is simply for powering on the unit. To its left is the micro-USB port, where the charge cord plugs in. The 3.5 mm headphone jack is on the left.

Questions to Ask Yourself About Your New Amazon Kindle Fire

Now that you have your new Kindle Fire, take the time to consider the following questions:

- *Where will you be using it?* The Amazon Kindle Fire is set up only for Wi-Fi. For those of you that plan to use the Kindle Fire at home on a secure network, this is a good thing. For those who plan to use the Kindle Fire in places with free Wi-Fi, such as coffee shops and libraries, this is not such a good thing. The last thing you want is someone getting into your private data through a back door on a public Wi-Fi, so it is wise not to look at online data you want secure. In other words, you don't want to access your online bank account in a public Wi-Fi area because someone might gain a back door into your account.

- *How well can you use it when offline?* If you are traveling by plane with the Kindle Fire, then you are going to be in many places where you won't have access to a Wi-Fi hot spot. Fortunately, there are many Android apps that do not require a Wi-Fi connection, not to mention all the content stored on the Kindle Fire device itself that you can read, hear, or watch while you are waiting to get online.

- *Should you get some kind of protective case?* Like any mobile device, you want to protect it from daily use. I highly recommend that you answer this question with a "yes." There are a lot of cases available that will protect the back and sides of your Kindle Fire from scuff marks and other scratches. Check out Chapter 3 for more information.

▪ *How much data do you intend to put on it?* You would be surprised at how quickly 8 GB of memory can get eaten up, especially when only 6 GB is usable and there is no expandable memory slot. A single, two-hour movie can occupy more than a gigabyte of storage, so that leaves space for only five to six films, at most. You can easily run out of memory if you like having video on the Fire. You might also want to carry around your pictures on your Kindle Fire; a typical photo is 300 KB to 1.2 MB. Amazon limited the amount of memory to keep the Kindle Fire price tag low; instead it offers customers cloud storage. The cloud is there for you, but you might want to get into a good habit of transferring content from the cloud to the device itself. Then you will want to free up space on the device later, or you might find yourself "full" when it comes to downloading the next thing that you want.

▪ *What other accessories will you need?* The Kindle Fire is meant to be taken with you whereever you go, but that doesn't necessarily mean that is ready for any trip as is. See Chapter 3 for more information on what accessories you might need.

Setting up Your Kindle Fire

You will need to follow the instructions on the card that comes with the Kindle Fire. First, connect the cord to the Kindle. After it is plugged in, hit the power button. The first thing you will see is the Welcome screen, as shown in Figure 1–4. This screen also shows how to connect to a network.

If you don't have a Wi-Fi network set up in your home, now is time to get one. I am assuming that you already have a home network, but if you don't, it is relatively simple to set it up. All that is required is connecting a router to your modem; routers are fairly cheap today. You will want to set up a network with a password so only you and those that you want on your network can access it.

Your home network should appear on the list shown on your Kindle Fire. If it doesn't, then your network might be having trouble, so check your connections and try again. If you can't get it to work, you can select another open network. I will explain in Chapter 2 how to set up your Kindle Fire for another local network, allowing you to use it in coffee shops, libraries, or any other place with an open Wi-Fi hot spot.

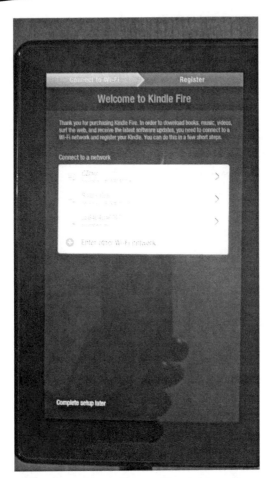

Figure 1–4. *The first thing you will see when you turn on your Kindle Fire.*

Once the network is connected, you should see a prompt asking you to select your time zone, as shown in Figure 1–5.

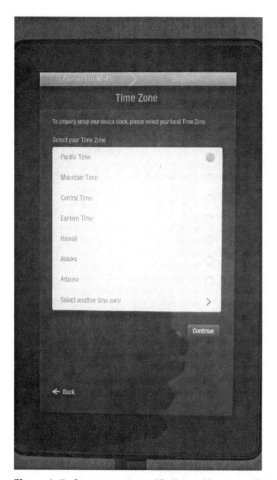

Figure 1–5. *Once you get your Kindle working, you will have to adjust for the proper time zone.*

You should see a quick flash of logging into your Amazon account. I already had an Amazon account when I set up my Kindle Fire, but if you don't have one, you can easily set up one by going to www.amazon.com. There you will find a link at the top of the screen that reads "New customer? Start here.". This leads you to the Amazom.com Sign In screen (see Figure 1–6).

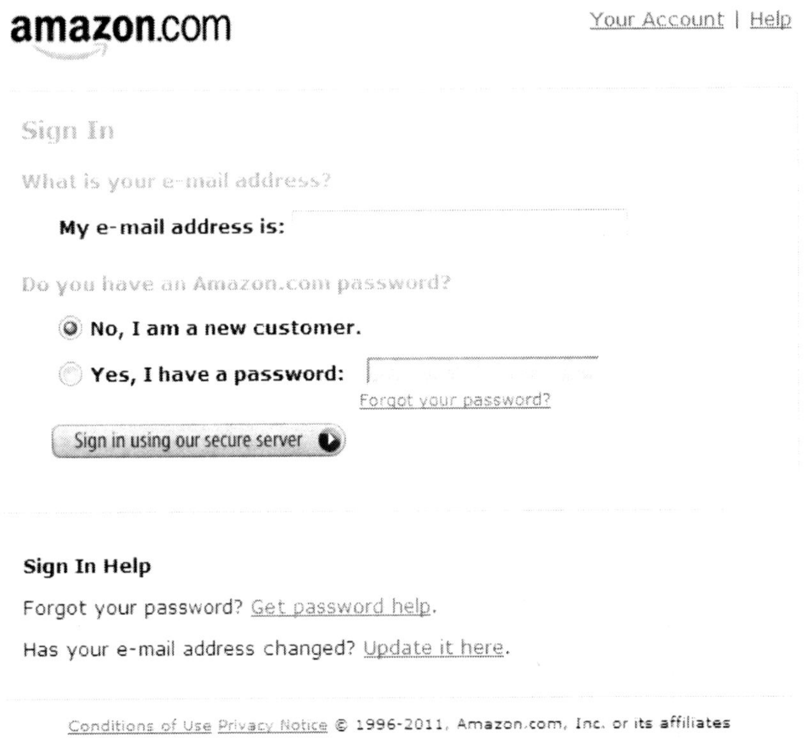

amazon.com
Your Account | Help
Sign In
What is your e-mail address?
My e-mail address is:
Do you have an Amazon.com password?
No, I am a new customer.
Yes, I have a password:
Forgot your password?
Sign in using our secure server
Sign In Help
Forgot your password? Get password help.
Has your e-mail address changed? Update it here.
Conditions of Use Privacy Notice © 1996-2011, Amazon.com, Inc. or its affiliates

Figure 1–6. *Setting up a new Amazon account is pretty simple. It is done at the Sign In screen.*

After the Kindle Fire verifies your Amazon account, you will see a screen that looks like Figure 1–7.

Welcome to Kindle Fire
Hello Mark Rollins. Not Mark Rollins?
Congratulations, your Kindle is registered!
The latest Kindle software is being downloaded. Once complete, it will only take a few minutes to restart your device and install the latest features.
Please connect your Kindle to the provided AC adapter to ensure you have sufficient battery charge to complete the process.

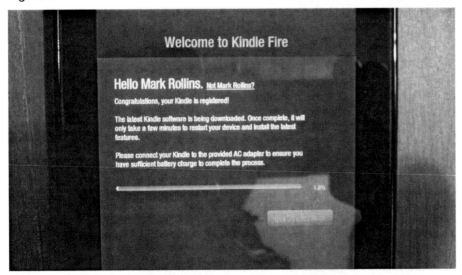

Figure 1–7. *After my Kindle is set up with a wireless network and an Amazon.com account*

It took more than fifteen minutes to download the updates. If it takes longer for you, that is pretty normal, so be patient. You should next see three screens offering tips (see Figure 1–8) before you finally get to the last screen.

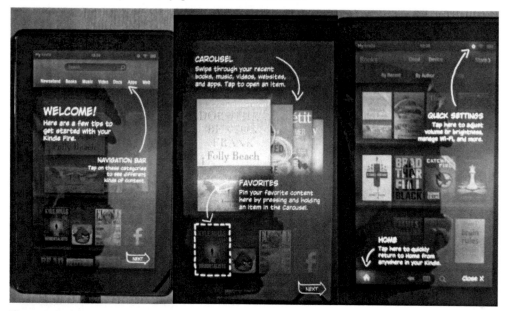

Figure 1–8. *A few screens offering tips*

Once you have sped past all those screens, you should receive the Home screen. I will go into detail on that in the next chapter.

Summary

One of the things that make Amazon such a popular company is that it gives its customers access to lots of content in all forms. The Kindle Fire, Amazon's first break into the tablet market, definitely creates a new way for consumers to get their books, music, and video content. For this reason, the Kindle Fire is poised to change the market for both tablets and e-readers.

Like any other high-priced purchase, you will want to make sure that everything you need is in the box and that the product as functioning at 100 percent efficiency. If not, you want to send it back right away.

You should ask yourself some important questions to reveal how you plan to use your Kindle Fire. One important question to ask is how much data you want on the Kindle Fire vs. how much you can actually put on the Kindle Fire. And you definitely need a home network set up if you plan on using it at home because the Kindle Fire is a Wi-Fi-only device.

Setting up the Kindle Fire can be done in mere minutes, but you need to give it permission to access your Amazon.com account. From there, you can begin downloading content and taking your Kindle Fire to the max!

Chapter 2

The Basics of the Kindle Operating System

Amazon really wanted to make certain that they had a winner on their hands with the Kindle Fire. Not only does it give the user access to millions of books, videos, and music, but the icing on the cake is the Android operating system.

The Rise of Android

Android was a start-up company that developed its own open-source operating system for mobile phones. It was purchased by Google in 2005. Shortly after Apple introduced the iPhone, Google wanted a new mobile operating system and started a consortium of companies known as the Open Handset Alliance (OHA). The OHA membership includes several major players in the mobile industry, including HTC, Samsung, Sprint, Motorola, and T-Mobile.

One of the reasons that Android is the operating system of choice on many tablets and smartphones is because it is open source. This means that users have the right to use, study, change, and improve its design through ready availability of the source code. This is different from the iOS Operating System on iPads and iPhones because it does not need to be tied to any particular device or manufacturer.

I can honestly say that I have loved working with Android ever since I purchased a Motorola Droid X, an Android phone. I would recommend trying an Android phone if you are a BlackBerry or iPhone user. In fact, I love Android so much, I have written a book about it entitled *The Business of Android Apps Development: Making and Marketing Apps that Succeed* (Apress, 2011).

But enough of me plugging my own work; let's get down to the basics of Android. The Home screen for the Kindle Fire and the one for an iPhone are quite similar. Then again, practically every user-friendly computer has programs that can open on the click of an icon. In the case of mobile operating systems, no mouse is required.

The Android Interface

If you press the home button on an iOS device, you will come to a home screen where you can examine all the apps with a finger swipe. Android on the Kindle Fire is very much the same; when you unlock the device or hit the Home button, you are taken to a single page that shows the available apps. The difference is in the arrangement, which I will explain later, but first, I want to quickly discuss two important tools of interface: the keyboard and screen orientation.

Figure 2–1. *The Amazon Kindle Fire Lock screen (left) and the Kindle Fire Home screen*

Your Kindle Fire Touchscreen Keyboard

Since the Kindle Fire doesn't have Bluetooth, you won't be able to hook up a Bluetooth keyboard to interface with it the way you can with other devices. You are stuck using the touchscreen keyboard.

Fortunately, the touchscreen keyboard is always there when you need it. All that is required is that you touch where you need to type, and the keyboard automatically appears. If you don't want the keyboard, no problem; just hit the Keyboard button in the lower-right corner (see Figure 2–2, left) and it will vanish. If you need to type numbers and symbols, you can hit the 123!? button in the lower-left corner (see Figure 2–2, right).

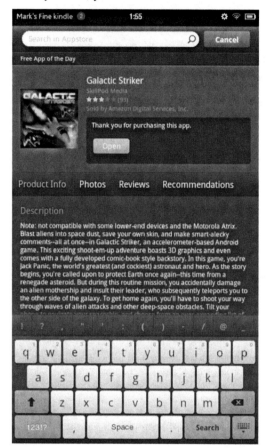 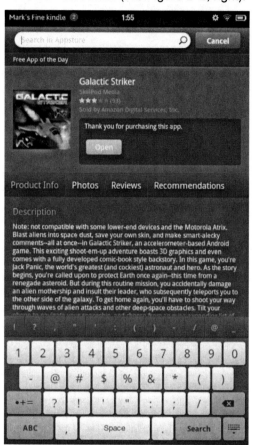

Figure 2–2. *The regular QWERTY keyboard (left) and the numerical/symbol keyboard (right)*

You might find that the touchscreen keyboard in portrait mode is very limited. If you rotate the Kindle Fire to landscape mode, the touchscreen surface is a little wider, making it feel more like a computer keyboard (see Figure 2–3).

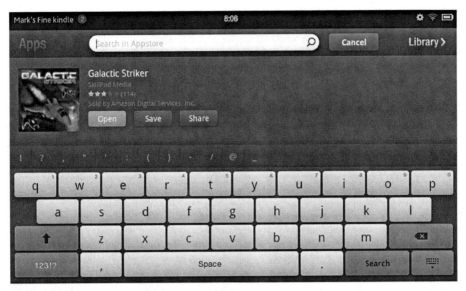

Figure 2–3. *The keyboard in landscape mode*

Screen Orientation

The Kindle Fire is set up for almost instantaneous changing from portrait to landscape view. Chances are you have already noticed that tilting it on its side will automatically orient the screen into landscape mode. The Kindle Fire remains in landscape mode until you shift it otherwise. Sometimes it seems to get stuck, and you have to do that "force-turn" in order to shift it into landscape or portrait. This is a plague that many devices have. For the sake of conserving space, I have chosen to show many of my screenshot illustrations in landscape mode, unless I can batch two together in portrait mode. It just saves space.

You will find that certain programs run best on the Kindle Fire in landscape mode, while others perform best in portrait. I have found that watching videos is much better in landscape because it uses all of the screen's real estate. I have found that some books and journals are best read in portrait mode. You decide what your Kindle Fire orientation will be.

The Kindle Fire's Version of Android

Android is a constantly-improving operating system. It receives updates to new versions periodically. At version 1.5, updates began being nicknamed after a sweet treat. This was more than just humor because each sweet treat is designated by a different letter. For example, version 1.5 is known as **C**upcake, version 1.6 is **D**onut, version 2.0/2.1 is **É**clair, and version 2.2 is **F**royo. If you are still confused about the naming scheme, look at the first letter of each name, in ascending alphabetical order.

The Amazon Kindle Fire comes with a modified version of Android 2.3, aka Gingerbread. While many Android users want the Kindle Fire to have version 3.0 (Honeycomb) or version 4.0 (Ice Cream Sandwich), it isn't available at this point.

In fact, I would not be surprised if the Kindle Fire never comes out with an upgrade of its current operating system. As you can tell by looking at the Home screen, the Kindle Fire is definitely designed as a content reader, not a screen that holds icons for apps, like most other Android devices.

There's No Place like Home Screen

Now that you have charged your Kindle, let's get into the fun of the Home screen, shown in landscape mode in Figure 2–4.

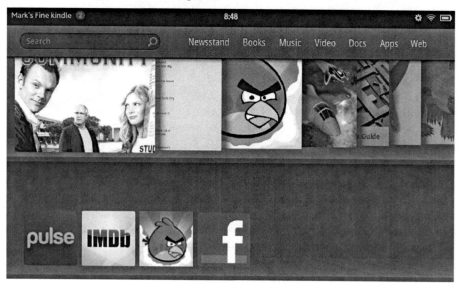

Figure 2–4. *My Home screen*

The following are a few things that you will notice about Kindle's Home screen, starting from the top of the screen and working down.

- *Notifications*: Located in the upper-left corner, it alerts you to messages from the system or apps. As you can see in Figure 2–4, I have two notifications waiting for me. Tapping this number shows me the notifications (see Figure 2–5). Tap Clear All to be rid of them. Eventually, it is worth it to clear your notifications, and tapping "Clear All" will get rid of them.

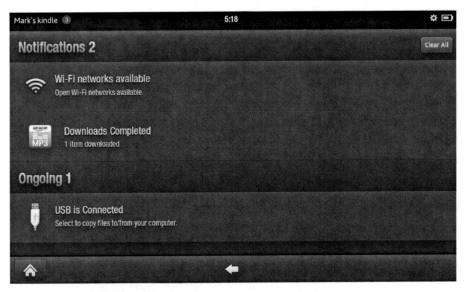

Figure 2–5. *The Notifications screen*

- *Time*: Located in the upper center of the screen, the time automatically sets when you download your updates, as detailed in Chapter 1. I will explain how to set time in the "Quick Settings" section later in this chapter.

- *Quick Settings*: Indicated by a cog icon in the upper-right corner. Tapping this icon results in a menu that I will later discuss in greater detail, but briefly, this menu covers locking and unlocking your screen rotation, adjusting volume, setting display brightness, accessing the Wi-Fi settings, syncing, and controlling the playback of music.

- *Wi-Fi Signal*: Located next to Quick Settings, it shows the strength of your Wi-Fi signal, indicated by the level that the bands are filled in. An X symbol means that you have access, but are currently not connected to the internet. I will explain how to log on to a wireless network later in the chapter, and a successful log-in will remove the "X".

- *Battery Indicator*: Indicated by a battery icon, the international symbol of power on a mobile device. It is difficult to tell exactly how powered the battery is, but it turns completely green when fully charged. When charging, the icon appears as a moving bar. If the battery power is low, its color changes to orange, which means you had better hurry up and charge that thing.

- *Search*: Searches your content libraries as well as the web. Tap here to type in your search. It resembles the famed Google or Yahoo search engines. It is helpful for finding content on your Kindle.

- *Navigation Bar*: Located underneath the search engine, the navigation bar takes you to your features. (I have devoted a chapter to each.) These include:

    - *Newsstand*: E-magazines and other online journals.

    - *Books*: E-books.

    - *Music*: Audio, in all kinds of formats.

    - *Video*: Video content, including that available on Amazon Prime.

    - *Docs*: Documents downloaded to the Kindle from a separate source.

    - *Apps*: Apps, including those downloaded from the Amazon Appstore for Android.

    - *Web*: Anything on the World Wide Web.

- *Carousel*: Stores and returns you to whatever you were most recently reading, listening to, or watching—books, music, videos, newspapers, magazines, web pages, and apps. These items are listed in chronological order, and you can swipe your finger to advance through them. Carousel occupies the largest amount of real estate on the Home screen. The first time you log in, you have a message from Jeff Bezos, Amazon.com CEO. I will explain more on how to navigate the Carousel later.

- *Favorites*: Allows you to easily access your favorite books, apps, and so forth. The default programs include Pulse, IMDB, and Facebook. Unlike the material on the Carousel, the icons in Favorites are meant for permanent storage, and they are user-defined. Like the Carousel, touching one of these icons opens the book, app, or whatever the type of program.

Opening a Program on the Home Screen

Like any other Android Home screen, accessing a program is as simple as touching the icon of the program. The only difference is that the icons on the Carousel and Favorites are quite large.

You might notice that it is possible to do a finger swipe on the Home screen and see that the bookshelf interface is quite large. While the Carousel is limited to horizontal scrolling, Favorites can hold seemingly infinite vertical shelf space.

I want to cover how the Carousel and Favorites relate.

The Carousel

If you have a book in the Carousel, it shows you how far you are from completion by a percentage in the corner (see Figure 2–6). If you press and hold the book thumbnail, you see that you have the option to Add to Favorites, or Remove from Carousel, or Remove from Device.

Figure 2–6. *Items on the Carousel*

If a music or video file is pressed and held, you usually get only the Add to Favorites or Remove from Carousel options. This doesn't mean that it cannot be deleted if you want to eliminate the file from your device.

It is important to note that if a journal or magazine is touched, Keep is an option. This is because individual issues of journals and magazines are automatically removed from the Kindle Fire after a certain amount of time, but you can choose to "keep" any issues that you want with this feature.

Next, I explain how the Favorites and the Carousel work together.

The Favorites

Pressing and holding an icon in Favorites allows you to choose whether or not you want to remove a program. Unlike the Carousel, the user can choose the order of the items by dragging and dropping. There is room on the Favorites shelf for many programs; shelf space is not limited, as shown in Figure 2–7.

I don't believe that there is a time limit on how long an item stays in the Favorites, so it is there when you need it.

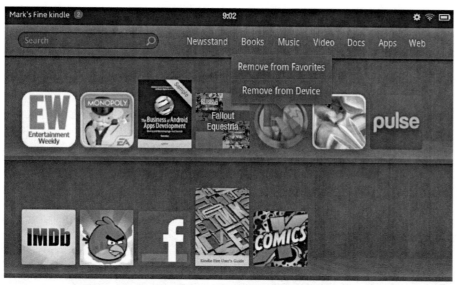

Figure 2–7. *If an item is already in Favorites, you see it on the bottom shelves. In this case, I have more than one shelf of favorites, but I can easily have more and can scroll down to view them all.*

The Control Buttons for the Kindle Fire

The first things you want to get familiar with on Android are the buttons. The iPhone and other iOS devices are famous for a one-button interface, since Apple likes to make things simple for users. Of course, we all know that it really is impossible to operate any complex hardware with one button, and using any application on an iOS device usually involves a lot of interesting finger swipes on menus within the app itself. Android applications are also complex, but I have found that the four-button standard makes things a whole lot easier to use.

The Kindle Fire also utilizes Android's four main buttons, as shown in Figure 2–8. The hard buttons are not on the device itself. To access them, just open any of the categories and do a finger swipe of the bottom of the screen. (These control buttons are not available on the Home screen.)

Figure 2–8. *The option bar, made visible by touching the bottom of the screen. The icons (from left to right) stand for Home, Back, Menu, and Search.*

These buttons are on most Android phones that are Gingerbread version or lower.

- *Home*: Takes you to the Home screen. It is similar to the one-button functionality of iOS devices.

- *Back*: Takes you back to the previous screen. If tapped enough times, it takes you to the Home screen.

- *Menu*: Finds additional options on an app or other type of program. Generally, if you can't figure out how to get a feature working on an app, you can find the answer here.

- *Search*: Brings up a search function on the application or program you are running, if the app/program offers this feature.

Knowing about Carousel, Favorites, and these four main control buttons are enough for you to get started accessing the categories on the navigation bar. The following section details the Quick Settings menu, which is very helpful for customizing your Kindle Fire.

The Quick Settings Menu

Tapping the cog icon in right corner of the Home screen opens the Quick Settings menu, which controls important aspects of your Kindle Fire. The six primary settings— Locked/Unlocked, Volume, Brightness, Wi-Fi, Sync, and More...—are shown in Figure 2–9.

Figure 2–9. *The six options available in Quick Settings; More... activates additional options*

Let's discuss these six settings.

- *Locked/Unlocked*: Controls the screen rotation. Sometimes the screen orientation is very inconvenient running certain applications. For example, I have noticed that rotating my Kindle Fire while on the Home screen resets the Carousel. You can keep your screen stable by tapping this setting to Locked. You can also get the screen Unlocked by tapping the same icon. Some programs, such as the video viewer, require that the Kindle Fire be in landscape mode, and they will function correctly even if you are locked in portrait mode.

- *Volume*: Controls the main volume of the Kindle Fire. Tapping Volume brings up an adjustable bar (as seen in Figure 2-9) so that you can make it as loud or as soft as you wish.

- *Brightness*: Brings up an adjustable control bar that makes the screen brighter or darker, depending on what you want.

- *Wi-Fi*: Allows you to turn off wireless networking or connect to another wireless network. Tap Wi-Fi and you get a screen like the one shown in Figure 2–10. From here, you can connect to a new network, just like you did during the initial startup of your Kindle Fire as described in Chapter 1..

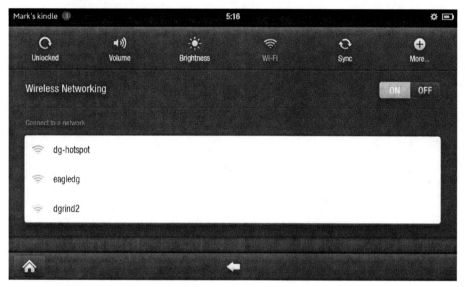

Figure 2–10. *Wirelessly connecting to the internet from the Quick Settings menu*

- *Sync*: Synchronizes your device with cloud content. You must be connected to the internet in order to sync.

- *More…*: Opens several additional ways to change the settings on your Kindle Fire (see Figure 2–11).

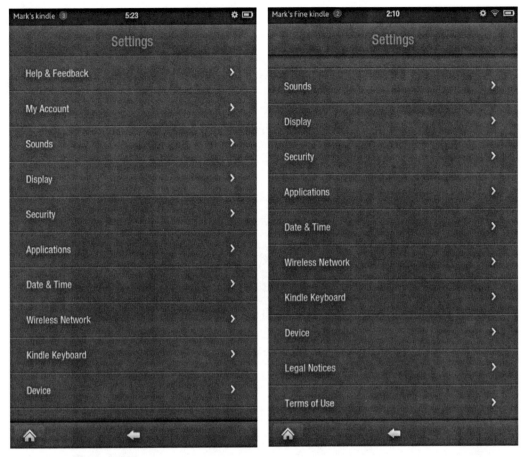

Figure 2–11. *More… settings*

Help & Feedback

Help & Feedback presents the user a screen with three different tabs. The first tab is FAQ & Troubleshooting, which is for handling minor Kindle Fire issues on your own (see Figure 2–12, left). Tapping any of the topics reveals a one-page help screen (see Figure 2–12, right).

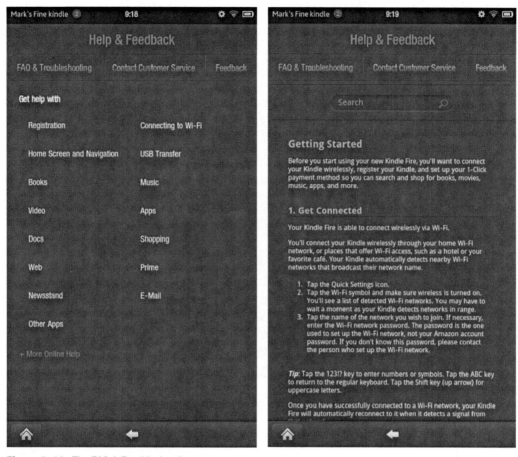

Figure 2–12. *The FAQ & Troubleshooting menu*

The second tab is for contacting Kindle customer service. It allows you to directly submit a question (see Figure 2–13, left). You receive a response via e-mail or phone. You can select help for several issues. Each issue has a list of frequently-asked questions (see Figure 2–13, right). If your question isn't on the list, you can type in your own, and then choose how you wish to be contacted with an answer.

I found this service helpful. I submitted a question just to see how long it would take to get an answer. I had a response in my e-mail box a few hours later. The response could have been from an automated system, but it was still a good answer and a testimony to how helpful this service can be.

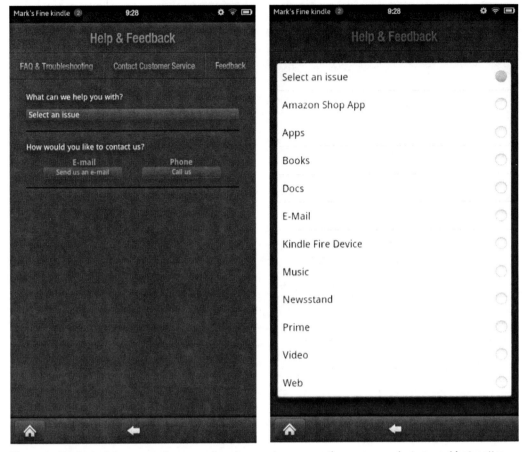

Figure 2–13. *Contact Amazon customer service when you have a question; you can select your subject matter from the checklist on the right.*

The third tab is for feedback. You select the feature you want to discuss and type in your thoughts about it (see Figure 2–14, left). You can choose from several features (see Figure 2–14, right) and rate them (one to five stars). Who knows, perhaps your comments will become integrated in the next version of the Kindle Fire, or could change the way the current version is handled now. This is your chance to complain or compliment.

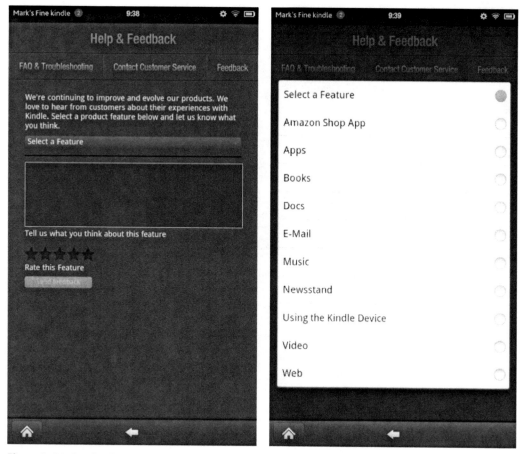

Figure 2–14. *Leaving feedback about your Kindle Fire (left), including a list of specific features to choose from*

My Account

Selecting My Account displays the account name under which your Kindle is registered (mine is shown in Figure 2–15). It also allows you to deregister your Amazon.com account. Oddly enough, it only seems to be accessible in portrait mode.

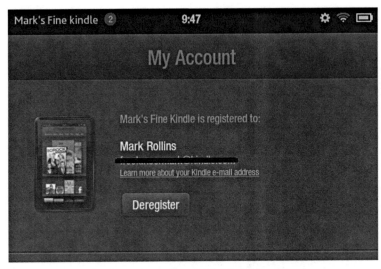

Figure 2–15. *The My Account page from the Quick Settings menu*

If you want to change your device name and e-mail address, it is done from Manage Your Kindle at www.amazon.com/myk. I will cover managing your account online many times in this book, but in case you are curious, a screenshot of the Manage Your Kindle page is shown in Figure 2–16.

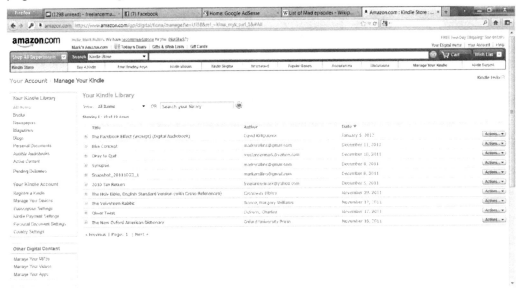

Figure 2–16. *The Manage Your Kindle account page at Amazon.com*

Restrictions

The Restrictions setting allows you to restrict the control of Wi-Fi access on your Kindle Fire (see Figure 2–17). When you select this setting, you are asked to activate a password, which is needed to activate Wi-Fi.

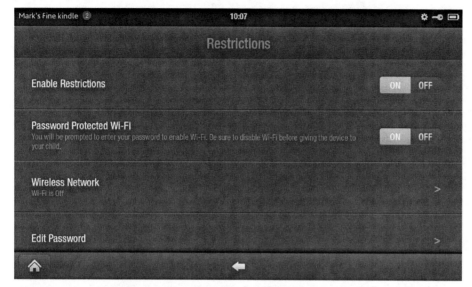

Figure 2–17. *The Restrictions screen allows you to password-protect your Kindle Fire Wi-Fi*

I have set up a password on my Kindle Fire, and although it is a little bit of a bother typing it in every time I go online, it is worth it to have this extra level of protection. I mentioned in Chapter 1 that using your Kindle Fire, a thief might be able to go online and access your financial information. The Restrictions option is an excellent method to prevent this access.

The only problem is if you forget your password, but you can reset your device to regain access. I will explain more about this soon.

Sounds

Not only does the Sounds setting allow control of the volume (see Figure 2–18), but you can also change the sound of incoming notifications. I won't bother trying to describe all the available sounds. Needless to say, they range from "Caffeinated Rattlesnake" to "Voila." You can sample all of the sounds. Have a good time listening.

Figure 2–18. *Adjust the volume and notification sounds in Sounds*

Display

Display allows you to control the brightness of your screen. It also lets you control the screen timeout (see Figure 2–19, left). The screen timeout allows you to choose the amount of time it takes before the screen times out to save battery life.

You can adjust time increments to be as low as 30 seconds or as high as one hour (see Figure 2–19, right). For those who want their Kindle Fire to remain on as long as possible, you should select Never, but know that this could drain battery life excessively with use.

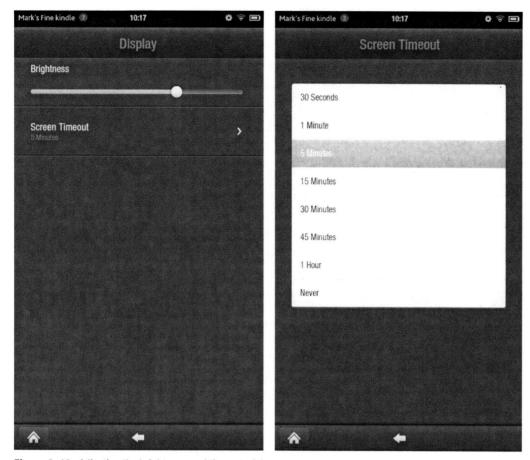

Figure 2–19. *Adjusting the brightness and timeout of the screen*

Your Kindle Fire goes into timeout mode after after your selected time increment if not used. This is one of those features designed to save battery life, but it can be inconvenient if you want the Kindle Fire to remain on for extended periods.

This setting won't affect the opening lock screen, which usually turns off in about a minute unless you choose to open it.

Security

Eventually, you put a lot information on your Kindle Fire that you don't want others to have. If your Kindle Fire is lost or stolen, you don't want to have anyone accessing your personal information. You should put a screen lock on it so that only you can access your Kindle Fire. This is done through the Security setting (see Figure 2–20, left). First you will need to select and set your Lock Screen password. It has to be at least four characters, with a confirmed entry (see Figure 2–20, right).

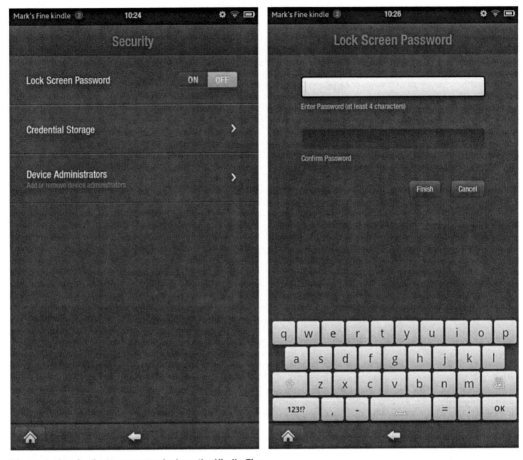

Figure 2–20. *Setting up a screen lock on the Kindle Fire*

It is also possible to set up device administrators and secure credentials here. Device Administrators lists the applications you have authorized to be device administrators for your phone, such as e-mail, calendar, or any other application that you have granted this authority to.

Secure Credentials allows applications to access your phone's encrypted store of secure certificates and related passwords, plus other credentials. This is helpful for VPN and Wi-Fi connections.

Applications

The Applications setting allows you to view your Kindle Fire applications, including those running and third-party apps (see Figure 2–21, left.) Selecting a single application gives you information about it, including the version, storage, and permissions (see Figure 2–21, right).

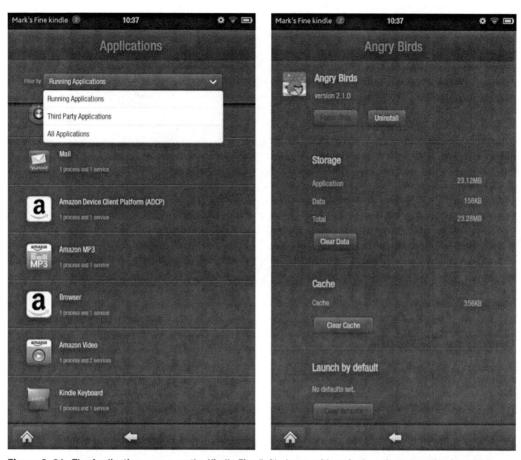

Figure 2–21. *The Applications menu on the Kindle Fire (left) shown with a single, selected application (right)*

Date & Time

The Kindle sets the time automatically while downloading updates, but if you want to set the time manually, just switch Automatic to Off and then tap Set Time or Set Date, as shown in Figure 2–22. Date & Time is also where you set your time zone.

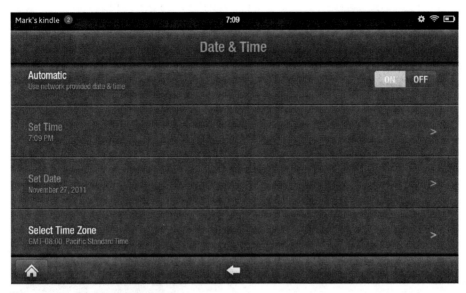

Figure 2–22. *Setting the date and time*

Wireless Network

The Wireless Network setting allows you to select your Wi-Fi network. It gives you a list of network options to select your connection, as shown in Figure 2–23.

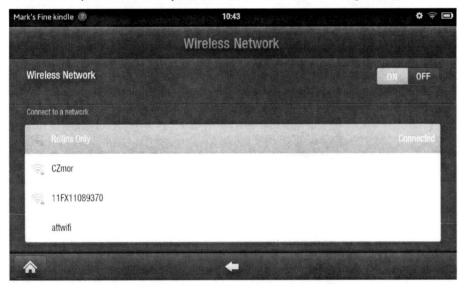

Figure 2–23. *My wireless network options*

Kindle Keyboard

If you want to make alterations to your keyboard, the Kindle Keyboard setting is where it happens (see Figure 2–24). The Sound on Keypress option allows the keyboard to make a noise while you type. Auto-capitalization gives you the choice to type in all caps or not. Quick Fixes corrects commonly typed mistakes.

Figure 2–24. *The Kindle keyboard settings*

Device

The Device page (see Figure 2–25) tells you how much memory you have in both the application and internal storage. It also shows how much power is left in the battery.

System Version tells you the version on your Kindle Fire. Updating it is as simple as tapping the Update button. This page also provides your specific serial number and Wi-Fi MAC address.

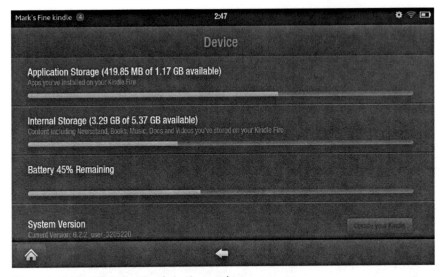

Figure 2–25. *The Device setting, in landscape view*

I will cover Allow Installation of Applications from Unknown Sources in Chapter 9. The Reset to Factory Defaults is one of those options you never tap unless you really mean it. It will remove your personal data and restore your Kindle Fire to default settings—the way it was when you first got it. This option removes all applications, books, magazines, videos, and anything else that you have purchased. This is a good option to have should you ever want to bring your Kindle Fire back to its original factory settings.

Legal Notice

The Legal Notice page provides the trademark, copyright, and other notices about the software installed on your Kindle.

Terms of Use

This page automatically directs the user to the Kindle License Agreement and Terms of Use on the web.

Summary

The Amazon Kindle Fire operates on the Android operating system. The Android operating system gives the user the freedom to access all of its features, as well as the Android Market.

The Android operating system is easy to use with its four-button controls. It is also easy to upgrade when a newer version is available. It is simple to customize; users can easily move applications to the Home screen, set their screen timeout, set up a screen lock, and make other adjustments.

Chapter **3**

Your Kindle Fire Daily Maintenance Plan

Even though many of us will claim that we "can't live" without our mobile devices, like cellular phones, tablets, cameras, and portable gaming stations, these devices often receive the worst treatment. It really is nothing personal; it's just that we mobile users never keep our devices in ideal conditions.

In addition to being jostled around repeatedly in our pockets, briefcases, and handbags, there is the occasional situation where a mobile device gets dropped or left out in bad weather. In the worst case scenario, our valuable devices get crushed.

Like any high-priced investment, you want to make certain that it is given proper maintenance so that it lasts as long as possible. Just as you need to maintenance your car every so often, you also need to maintain your Kindle Fire.

After all, the Kindle Fire is going to give you access to a lot of content. Its Android operating system with its many applications has the potential to make you very productive. The least you can do is treat the Kindle Fire with respect. Think of it as a controlled fire in a fireplace; it needs proper maintenance to keep it going.

Treat Your Kindle Fire Like You Treat Your Mobile Phone

Think of how you treat your mobile phone. Chances are it's at your bedside to wake you with its alarm function or app. From there, you probably take it to work, bringing the charger with you so you can give it some juice in a spare outlet by your desk. You may have some sort of car adapter so you can charge your phone on your daily commute.

You probably use your phone off and on at work, maybe when you are supposed to use your landline business phone. You may have noticed that the phone works better when it is set up to work with a Wi-Fi hot spot rather than off the cellular phone dataplan. So you might switch to Wi-Fi, just to preserve battery life.

As you go through your day, you probably use your phone and its applications for all sorts of work- (and non-work) related activities. You then probably take it home and use it at night. You may even use it for gaming or watching videos.

My point is that we have put a lot of importance in our mobile devices. The more you use your Kindle Fire, the more you won't want to be without it. Eventually, it will become a part of your daily routine.

Your Kindle Fire Daily Routine

Like your phone, you might want to keep your Kindle Fire by your bedside. It is perfect for watching videos or reading before bed, and the long battery life keeps it from running out. You can also use the Kindle Fire as an alarm if you find the proper app, and there are many.

You will find many reasons for taking the Kindle Fire to work with you. After all, you will find that you can download many work-related books, journals, and videos. You will be able to do many things with it, even without a Wi-Fi access point. Chances are you will soon develop a routine of finding hot spots on your commute to work, just so you can use your Kindle Fire. For example, you might find that a bus stop or subway stop has a Starbucks nearby and you can access their free Wi-Fi. That five or ten minutes of free Wi-Fi may be the most productive of your commute.

As you program your Kindle Fire for your personal Wi-Fi network, home will become your "fortress of solitude" as your Kindle Fire lives to its full potential online.

Cloud vs. Device Storage

Even though I have talked about basics in the first two chapters, I haven't really spent much time talking about storage on the Kindle Fire. You will notice on such categories, that Cloud and Device are at the top of the screen, as if it is incredibly important. This is because it is extremely important. You will discover the fun game of cloud vs. device to access your content. According to the *Kindle Fire User's Guide*, "Content purchased from Amazon is securely stored by Amazon and available in the cloud." Then comes the most important piece of advice: "If you are preparing to go offline, toggle to Cloud and download to your device content that you want to have available when offline."

Content Is King

You might remember that I discussed how Amazon might actually be losing money on the Kindle Fire because the cost to make it is higher than the price to sell it. This is because Amazon hopes to offset costs through the purchase of content. As someone who owns a Kindle Fire, I can tell you that I have spent more money on its content than I had ever spent at Amazon before.

Amazon appears to want me to spend more. I recently received an e-mail from the company (see Figure 3–1), inviting me to enjoy the "unlimited space for your music in Cloud Drive + 20 GB of storage for your other files for just $20 each year." An offer like that definitely gives me the opportunity for unlimited music storage, and 20 GB for everything else.

amazon.com   Your Amazon.com   Digital Deals   Follow us:

Dear Amazon.com Customer,

Right now, you can get unlimited space for your music in Cloud Drive + 20 GB of storage for your other files for just $20 each year. With that, you can back up your entire music library securely - then enjoy that music wherever you are, on your Kindle Fire, computer, or Android device.

Still growing your music collection? Don't miss some of our favorite one-hit wonders - just $0.69 for a limited time. Purchases saved to the cloud won't count towards your storage limit.

amazon cloud player

Learn more about Cloud Player

Figure 3–1. *You might have received this offer by Amazon for unlimited music on your Cloud Player. If you want unlimited music storage, it is a good deal.*

You might have to develop a new discipline for purchasing content for your Kindle Fire. You also have to develop a cloud vs. device discipline. The Amazon Cloud is terrific for storing all your content, and it can store quite a lot of things. Sadly, the Kindle Fire is limited to just a Wi-Fi hot spot connectivity. If you have access to a Wi-Fi hot spot, then you have unlimited access to the cloud and, therefore, all your content.

Without the cloud access, you only have device access. Therefore, take advantage of a hot spot and move content from the cloud to the device if you know that you are going to access it later without a hot spot. For example, if you know that you want to view content on the bus ride to work tomorrow, be certain to download it to the device from the cloud today. Having content on the device will make long rides easier as you will have something to do.

The discipline of moving content from cloud to device will become as everyday as charging your Kindle Fire. Eventually, you will find the 6 GB worth of device memory to be like gold and be very choosy about what you store on it. You will find that there are songs, books, journals, and videos that you can do without during periods where hot spots are not available.

Accessories for Your Kindle Fire

You will want to invest in accessories that protect the Kindle Fire from simple, daily usage. This can be as simple as external protection, as well as practical products that make usage easier.

A Protective Case

Life happens to mobile devices: drops, extended stays in the pocket, and other daily use. I highly recommend a protective case. I wouldn't dare purchase any touchscreen device unless I could also purchase a protective case for it.

There are a lot of cases available that protect the back and sides of your Kindle Fire from scuff marks and other kinds of bumps and scratches. I suggest a folio model that provides a level of protection on the front by closing up the Kindle Fire like it's in a folder.

A search on the Amazon site for "Kindle Fire Case" turns up several cases, including some from Marware, rooCASE, and Splash. I recently got a chance to try out one from Belkin called the Verve Folio Stand (see Figure 3–2). Not only does it provide fold-up, folio-style protection, but it also works as a stand.

Figure 3–2. *The Belkin Verve Folio Stand. Not only does it protect your Kindle Fire from scratches, but it props it up, as well.*

Kindle Screen Protector

The Kindle Fire screen is made of Gorilla Glass, which is designed to be quite tough and scratch free. I have seen videos of cellular phones with Gorilla Glass, and they often show the screen easily surviving a blow from a hammer. In January 2012, Corning, the manufacturer, announced the release of Gorilla Glass 2, which is even stronger. I wouldn't be surprised if this stronger type ended up on the next version of the Kindle Fire.

According to the official *Kindle Fire User's Guide*, "The glass could break if the device is dropped or receives a substantial impact." I honestly don't want to know what would cause such a break, and the user's guide warns not to touch or attempt to remove the damaged glass.

The first problem that you notice with any device that has a touchscreen is how easily it attracts fingerprints and other types of smudges. This is especially true when you have young children who love to get a hold of touchscreen devices.

You want to invest in a screen protector to shield the touchscreen from fingerprints and smudges. Many screen protectors do not hinder functionality and are easy to apply. Keep in mind that you have to change them every so often and that they should be disposed of properly to protect the environment.

I highly recommend putting a screen protector on your Kindle Fire screen before you touch it for the first time. The one shown in Figure 3–3 is the Splash Masque Screen Protector Matte, which is made specifically for the Kindle Fire.

Figure 3–3. *The Splash Masque Screen Protector Film Matte, a thin piece of plastic designed to protect the Kindle Fire.*

There are a lot of companies that create screen protectors that guard the entire device. ZAGG's invisibleSHIELD is one that I have seen work on other mobile devices. Figure 3–4 shows the one available for the Kindle Fire.

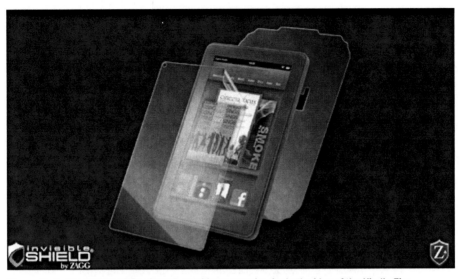

Figure 3–4. *The ZAGG invisibleSHIELD provides protection for both sides of the Kindle Fire*

ZAGG demonstrates its invisibleSHIELD by putting a mobile device inside a box filled with screws and then shaking the box. That is enough to cover any device full of scratches, but the invisibleSHIELD protects the device from any harm. I have seen this test at trade conventions; it is enough to show that this product is more than adequate for protecting a mobile device.

Although you are guarding the screen with the protectors, you also might want to buy special cleaning wipes. I had a chance to try out the Kimtech Touchscreen Cleaning Wipes (see Figure 3–5). I found that these inexpensive wipes cleared my Kindle Fire of smudges. You should probably give your screen a good wipe-down before you put on a protector of any type.

I recently used a Kimtech wipe on my Kindle Fire after a month's worth of use without a screen protector. I found that the Kimtech Touchscreen Cleaning Wipe turned the screen into something nigh virginal.

Figure 3–5. *Kimtech's Touchscreen Wipes provide a good way to clean a Kindle Fire's touchscreen.*

A Kindle Stand

I know that a lot of people purchase a Kindle Fire specifically for viewing video content, which it does well, as I will detail in later chapters. It is good to stand your Kindle Fire at an angle to watch video content like a television.

Back when the iPad first came out, there were a lot of companies that realized that people would want a stand. One of the cheapest available was a business card holder that cost less than a dollar, while some stands sold for more than $120.

The Stump Stand (see Figure 3–6) is a low-cost alternative. It is a heavy disc with a slot designed for standing a tablet PC at an angle for viewing in portrait or landscape mode.

Figure 3–6. *The Stump Stand, a low-priced device designed for holding up a Kindle Fire*

Stylus

There are some touchscreen users that have never touched their screen; this is because they have invested in a conductive stylus. I guarantee a stylus will keep your screen quite smudge-free. Some protective cases come with a slot for the stylus to help prevent it from becoming lost.

Keep in mind that the stylus must be conductive, which means that the touchscreen will have to accept it like a finger. The stylus from the Nintendo DS, for example, will not be adequate; neither is an ordinary pen or stick.

I recently got a chance to try out a stylus that is also a ballpoint pen and a laser pointer. It is the Stylus + Pen + Laser Pointer from Griffin Technologies, shown in Figure 3–7.

Figure 3–7. *The Stylus + Pen + Laser Pointer from Griffin Technologies*

Note that the stylus tip of this particular model is quite thick, but there are thinner styluses to enable you to make precise touches. When using a touchscreen, it is easy to conceal things with your fingertip. And, the smaller the button, the greater the chance for your fingertip to miss it.

A stylus is also helpful when you are using your Kindle Fire in cold weather. Despite the name, the Fire won't keep you warm, and you cannot use a touchscreen with gloves unless they are specially-made gloves. A stylus, however, can be used with regular gloves.

Touchscreen Gloves

I recently discovered a pair of touchscreen gloves known as Agloves. They have patent-pending technology that "harnesses the body's natural bioelectricity from the surface of the entire hand by using silver, the most conductive element on the Periodic Table of Elements." This silver is knit in all the ten fingers, so you can access the touchscreen in many ways. Figure 3–8 shows the Agloves being used on an iPhone, but they work just as well on a Kindle Fire.

Figure 3–8. *Agloves, a pair of gloves that protect your hands from cold weather, but still give you access to your touchscreen. Go to www.agloves.com for more information.*

Power Adapter

If you are planning to take your Kindle Fire with you as you travel the world, you are going to want to bring an adapter that can handle all of the world's outlets. For example, European voltage is twice what American voltage is, and the plugs are different. The Kindle Fire's instructions state that it supports 100–240 volts.

BoxWave (www.boxwave.com) sells an international outlet plug adapter kit, as shown in Figure 3–9. You should visit the company's web site to take a look at their other Kindle Fire products, as well.

Figure 3–9. *An international outlet plug adapter kit from BoxWave for those who intend to travel worldwide with their Kindle Fire (it comes in handy for other electronic goods, as well)*

An External Battery

The Kindle Fire battery life is pretty good for about eight hours. I would highly suggest to first charge it to its fullest, and then use it with the battery. Wait until it is almost completely drained before charging it again. Most devices should not be constantly charged because it makes them dependent on constant power to function.

If you have any experience with mobile devices, then you know how they have a tendency of running out of power, especially when you most need them. For this reason, I keep an external battery on me to give my smartphone the extra juice it needs in case I need to make an important call.

There are also external batteries for the Kindle. Figure 3–10 shows the 8000mAh external battery for the Amazon Kindle Fire; it comes with additional connectors for other devices. I found that anything with a micro-USB port connector will do. As long as you remember to keep it charged and with you, you have that extra power available when necessary.

Figure 3–10. *The 8000mAh external battery for Amazon Kindle Fire.*

While I am on the subject of external batteries, I want to discuss the internal battery and how the user's guide recommends that it only be charged within a temperature range of 32 to 95 degrees Fahrenheit (0 to 35 degrees Celsius).

USB to Micro-USB Connector

If you want content loaded onto your Kindle Fire from an outside source like your computer, you need a USB to micro-USB connector. I have no idea why Amazon did not include one with the Kindle Fire as a standard; it wouldn't have been too difficult to include one that could separate from the outlet plug in the wall, like my mobile phone. I'm sure that there is a good reason. You should be able to get an Amazon Basics brand (see Figure 3–11) at Amazon.com. I will discuss more about how to use this connector in Chapter 8.

I discovered that attaching my Kindle Fire to my computer seems to give the Kindle more power, even though I do not see the battery indicator charging in any way. I'm not certain if this is just my perception, but it appears that my Kindle Fire seems to last longer with a charging cable.

Figure 3–11. *A modestly-priced micro-USB to USB cable available from Amazon Basics*

External Speakers

Those that want to use the Kindle Fire for its music and video capabilities might want to invest in stereo speakers. All that is required is a set that can plug into the headphone jack.

iPod and iPad docks are a huge market for Apple's products, and there are an increasing number of speaker-oriented products made for the Kindle Fire. For example, Nyko, a company famous for its video-game accessories, recently started making a whole slough of Kindle Fire products, one of them being the Speaker Stand, shown in Figure 3–12.

Figure 3–12. *Nyko's Speaker Stand, made for the Kindle Fire to increase the external speaker sound*

Nyko also makes other products for the Kindle Fire, such as an adapter kit and a protective case.

Should the Worst Happen

The worst thing that can happen to your Kindle Fire happens to several thousand cell phones per day: they get dropped in the toilet. You may discover that it is a pleasure to view content on the Kindle Fire while relaxing in the bathtub. I don't think I need to discuss the downside of that. It isn't pretty, for so many reasons.

Water Damage

The *Kindle Fire User's Guide* states to do the following if the device gets wet: "unplug all cables, turn off the wireless, and let the screen revert to the screen saver. Wait for the device to dry completely before pressing the Power button to wake again. Do not attempt to dry your Kindle Fire with an external heat source, such as a microwave oven or hair dryer."

I have never had the misfortune of dropping my Kindle Fire or any other mobile device in water, but if I did, I would probably try something to effectively dry it out. For example, a product known as the BHEESTIE Bag (see Figure 3–13) claims that is able to dry out soaked mobile devices. It does this using BHEESTIE beads, which have the ability to draw out water from a damaged device. It is similar to the method of drying out a wet cellular phone in a cup of uncooked dried rice placed in a plastic bag.

Figure 3–13. *BHEESTIE Bag, what is needed for a wet Kindle Fire*

Whatever the case, make certain that you have some sort of insurance should the unfortunate "just add water" fate happens to your Kindle Fire.

Theft

Someone once asked me a difficult question: Which would you rather lose, your mobile or your wallet? In this age, we don't want a stranger using our mobile phone any more than we want a thief to have our wallet. I can think of a lot of problems that can happen if someone has my mobile phone, as he or she could probably figure out how to access my accounts. In the same way, most of us will have a lot of important information on our

Kindle Fire. While its one-touch shopping might make it easy for us to purchase books, e-journals, music, and video, a thief can take advantage of this, quite easily.

Should your Kindle Fire become lost or stolen, then your first course of action should be to deregister your account. This can be accomplished at any internet-connected computer from the Manage Your Kindle page on Amazon.com (amazon.com/manageyourkindle). Locate your device, click the Deregister link, and click the Deregister button in the pop-up window. A confirmation message appears above the device name on the Manage Your Devices page.

A deregistered Kindle cannot access Whispernet, so no one can use the Kindle's web function for purchases. Considering that very vital financial information can be snagged from a Kindle Fire, deregistering is essential to keep financial records safe.

Summary

You should invest in protection for and maintenance of your Kindle Fire. A case or folio-style case can protect it quite well. Do not underestimate the value of a screen guard; it can do a world of good when it comes to protection against smudges.

There are other accessories that also help the Kindle Fire user. They include a stylus, a stand, a micro-USB to USB cable, an external battery, and a power adapter.

In case your Kindle Fire gets dropped in water, you should have a plan for removing the moisture from it, like using the BHEESTIE Bag. Also have a plan in case your Kindle Fire is lost or stolen; know how to deregister your Kindle.

Taking precautions with certain accessories can help make certain that your Kindle Fire is used to its full potential and insure a long life for the user.

Chapter 4

Newsstand

I am old enough to remember when some magazines were still printed in black and white. That seems so antique now, as most magazines are in full color. But this is how Kindle users have been looking at magazines until now. The Kindle Fire brings magazines to the user in full color, and it is very welcome.

The Newsstand Feature of the Kindle Fire could very well be a game-changer when it comes to traditional magazines and newspapers. You might want to consider whatever finances you use on print media and spend it on digital media on the Newsstand. Chances are you will probably save money.

In this section, you will learn to search the Newsstand for the electronic magazine or newspaper that you are looking for. You will also learn how to purchase the e-journal, and how it is set up for reading. You'll find that the screen of the Kindle Fire is much smaller than most magazine and newspaper pages, but what it may lack in size, it makes up in resolution. The Newsstand has features like word searching, which, of course, is not available with print magazines.

Some magazines are only available as applications, with a subscription price. The good news is that Amazon Kindle Fire users can also manage their magazine subscriptions online from any internet-connected computer.

Your Kindle Fire Newsstand

The first thing that you notice when you open the Newsstand on your new Kindle Fire is that it is a completely blank shelf (see Figure 4–1, left). Unlike the Books or Docs section, Amazon doesn't include any default magazines with your purchase.

Normally, magazines and newspapers are put on a virtual shelf, arranged like they would be on a real newsstand. About the only thing worth noting at this point about the empty Newsstand shelf is the control buttons on the bottom and the access to the Store in the upper-right corner. Tapping on Store will open it (see Figure 4–1, right).

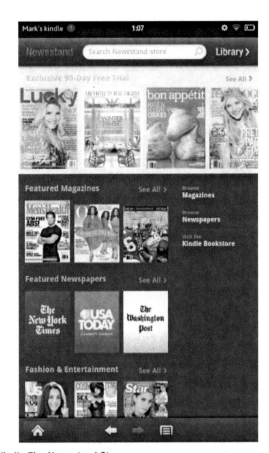

Figure 4–1. *The Kindle Fire Newsstand, along with the Kindle Fire Newsstand Store*

As you can see in Figure 4–1, there are several magazines on the top shelf that offer an exclusive 90-day free trial. Under these 90-day trial magazines are the featured magazines, followed by the featured newspapers. Under Fashion & Entertainment are various other journals.

If you touch Exclusive 90-Day Free Trial, you see a scrollable list of magazines available for free 90-day trial (see Figure 4–2). Note that some are labeled Page View Enabled. This means that you have a page view of the magazine that is the same as viewing it in print; I will go more into detail on those benefits later in this chapter.

As you continue to scroll down, you see that some magazines are available as apps, which I will also discuss later in this chapter. The ones that are apps are usually labelled "Free" and "Subscription may be required".

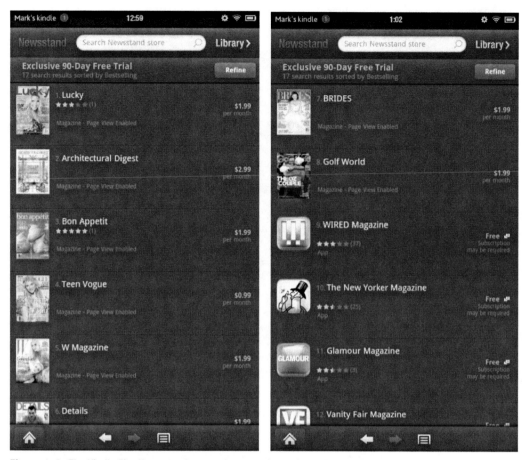

Figure 4–2. *The Kindle Fire Newsstand screen for magazines with a 90-day trial*

I'm sure that the list of available magazines has changed since this writing, but let's say you are interested in *W Magazine*, and so you tap on it; you then see a window like the one shown in Figure 4–3.

Figure 4–3. *The Newsstand store entry for* W Magazine, *where you can subscribe to or buy the current issue*

As you can see from Figure 4–3, the publisher (Condé Nast) is listed, along with the circulation (monthly). Scroll down and note the description, as well as the Customers Who Bought This Item Also Bought section on related journals. If you want to read customer reviews, then you need to scroll down further.

You should also note that current issue prices are more expensive than the monthly price. With a current issue of *W Magazine* costing $4.99 and a subscription price of $1.99 per issue, it is a good idea to subscribe if you plan to read one more than one issue.

Let's say that you want to subscribe to this magazine, or at least get on the free 90-day trial. Go ahead and tap on the Subscribe Now. The transaction takes place immediately and you have access to your magazine once it finishes downloading. On this particular page, the orange Subscribe Now button becomes a green Read Now; if you tap on it, you can read your magazine.

Reading a Magazine on the Kindle Fire

Figure 4–4 shows magazine pages ready for you to read on your Kindle Fire.

Figure 4–4. *Reading a magazine on the Kindle Fire in portrait mode*

As you can see in Figure 4–4, the bottom of the display is a scroll bar that essentially lets you navigate through all the pages in the magazine—page by page—including the cover. Scrolling along these pages causes them to move slowly, but the sliding bar underneath allows browsing the pages at a greater speed. Touching any of the thumbnail pages brings up that particular page for reading. The scroll bar closes if you touch anywhere else on the page.

Let's read in landscape view. In Figure 4–5, notice that pages 53 and 54 are merged in landscape view, whereas they were not in portrait. Landscape view is more like reading a magazine, even if the views are smaller.

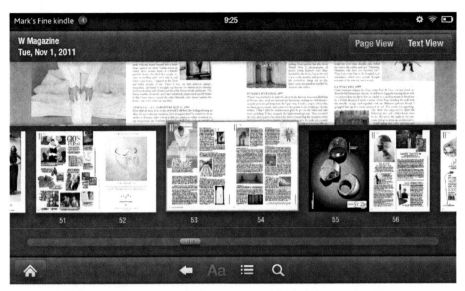

Figure 4–5. *Reading a magazine in landscape view on the Kindle Fire*

I am sure you already know that the pages in a magazine can be "turned" using finger swipes along the left or right side of the page; you swipe on the right to go forward, and swipe on the left to go back a page. The pinch-to-zoom feature works well for viewing close-ups of magazine content, and you may have to use it in order to read text.

The menu bar on the bottom of the display provides a few options. The Home button takes you to the Kindle Fire Home screen and the Back button returns you to wherever you were most recently. I will explain the "Aa" Text button and the magnifying glass Search button later in this chapter, but next I will talk about the Contents button.

The Table of Contents

Tapping the Contents button will open a Table of Contents that shows you where to find the articles in a journal (see Figure 4–6). Touching any article will take you to that particular article.

Figure 4–6. *Accessing the Table of Contents, which is easy to do on a Kindle Fire*

By the way, the Table of Contents can identify articles within sections of magazines. You know how some magazines have sections that are nothing more than a series of news blurbs? The Kindle Fire Table of Contents feature can take you to a blurb with a touch of a finger.

Searching a Magazine

Like the Home screen, the Kindle Fire Newsstand has a search engine that can find a word or keywords. All that is required is tapping the magnifying glass and typing the word(s) to search. The search is only done within the context of the particular magazine, so it is not searching the web or any of the other media on your Kindle Fire (you want to use the Home screen search engine for that).

Figure 4–7 shows what happened when I did a search on the word "diamond" in the December 2011 issue of *W Magazine*.

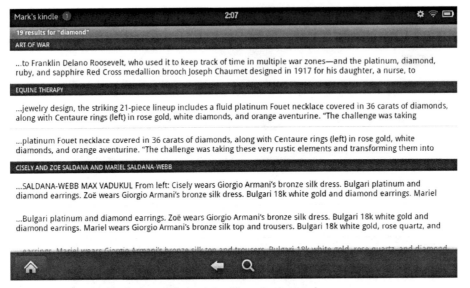

Figure 4–7. *The results of a keyword search in a Newsstand magazine*

A search on "diamond" yielded 19 results with that issue. Tapping on any one of these results instantly takes you to the entry within the magazine. First, however, you are alerted that you must switch to Text View.

Page View vs. Text View

Page View is good for reading articles as they would appear in the print version of a magazine; but sometimes that print looks very small on the Kindle Fire, and you might tire of using the pinch-to-zoom to read.

If the words (not the pictures) in the magazine are your focus, then you should access the Text View, which primarily provides the text of the article—giving the look and feel of a book on the Kindle Fire.

Switching from Page View to Text View is as simple as tapping on the selection in the upper-right corner of the screen. You can see the differences between Page View and Text View in Figure 4–8.

Figure 4–8. *A magazine article in Page View (left) and in Text View (right)*

Occasionally, the Text View will include a picture from the Page View, as shown in Figure 4–8. Note that the one-page article in Page View is six pages in Text View, and that the Text View has convenient buttons for turning pages at the bottom of the screen.

In Text View, a button labeled "Aa" suddenly becomes active in the menu bar. This is the Text button. Figure 4–9 shows what happens when you press the Text button in landscape mode.

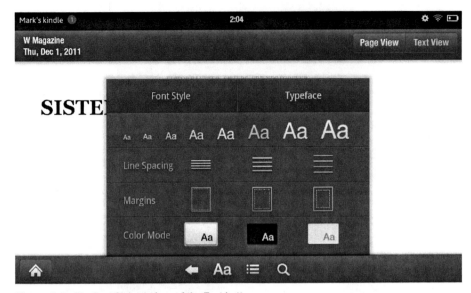

Figure 4–9. *The Font Style choices of the Text button*

The Text button allows you to select the Font Style and Typeface that you want to read in. Typeface options include the following:

- Georgia
- Caecilia
- Trebuchet
- Verdana
- Arial
- Times New Roman
- Courier
- Lucida

Font Style includes the following options:

- *Size*: Resizes the letters larger or smaller to make it easier for you to read.
- *Line Spacing*: If you are more comfortable with more space between the lines, then you will want to choose this option.
- *Margins*: This brings in the page with bigger margins on each side.
- *Color Mode*: This allows you to change the color of the "paper" that the text is "printed" on. If you want white print on a black background—you can do that! Another option is a tan color that looks similar to that of older books.

Using the Newsstand Search Engine to Find a Magazine or Newspaper

Let's explore the Newsstand search engine to find some of your favorite magazines. Figure 4–10 shows a quick search that I did to find magazines on technology.

Figure 4–10. *What a quick search on "technology" reveals on the Kindle Newsstand search engine*

Considering that the Kindle Fire has access to over 1,000 journals online, you should easily find some of your favorites. Some magazines and newspapers have free trials, so you can decide whether or not you want to subscribe. You definitely want to keep track of what you subscribed to and when the trial period has ended, or you might end up paying for subscriptions that you do not want. I will talk about how to manage your subscriptions later in the chapter; but next, I want to discuss newspapers.

Purchasing a Newspaper on the Kindle Fire

Purchasing a newspaper on the Kindle Fire is quite similar to purchasing a magazine (many newspapers also offer trial deals). Figure 4–11 shows an entry for *The New York Times*.

Figure 4–11. *The entry for* The New York Times *on the Kindle Fire Newsstand*

As you can see in Figure 4–11, the buttons and descriptors are almost identical to that of a magazine entry, including the option of buying a subscription or a current issue. If you take the subscription price (monthly) vs. the current issue price, you will find that it is significantly cheaper to subscribe for a month than to purchase one digital copy per day.

Reading a Newspaper on the Kindle Fire

One difference between reading a newspaper and a magazine on the Kindle Fire is that rather than a cover page, a newspaper begins with something that looks like a Table of Contents (see Figure 4–12).

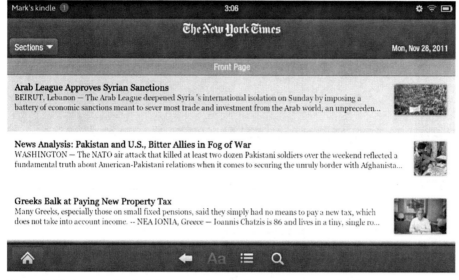

Figure 4–12. *An example of what you see after opening a newspaper on the Newsstand*

Selecting the Sections button (located in the upper-left corner), allows you to scroll to the section that you want to read (see Figure 4–13). Touching the section of your choice brings you a list of that section's current articles.

Figure 4–13. *Tapping the Sections button shows the sections available in the newspaper's current edition*

.Newspapers don't have a Page View—most articles look like the Text View format in magazines. And if a newspaper article has a picture associated with it, you can see it (see Figure 4–14).

THE ARTS SPIDER-MAN, A YEAR AFTER FIRST PREVIEW, IS ON SOLID

'Spider-Man,' a Year After First Preview, Is on Solid Ground

Chad Batka for The New York Times

Reeve Carney, center, star of "Spider-Man," with fellow Spider-Men on 42nd Street on Thanksgiving. After a dramatic path to Broadway, the show makes more than its operating costs weekly.

By PATRICK HEALY

One year after naysayers were predicting

a quick death, the musical "Spider-Man: Turn Off the Dark" is doubling down on Broadway, forgoing potentially lucrative overseas tours in the near term to try to refine the New York production and burnish the long-term value of the show.

In an interview to mark the Monday anniversary of the production's first, fumbling preview performance, the producers of "Spider-Man" said they were considering new plans for recouping the show's record-setting $75 million capitalization. The most unusual idea: adding new scenes and perhaps a new musical number to the New York "Spider-Man" every year, making it akin to a new comic book edition, and then urging the show's fans to buy tickets again.

The producers are also expanding to all

Figure 4–14. *A newspaper article on the Kindle Fire*

Other than that, reading a newspaper on the Kindle Fire is just like reading a magazine, and the Search, Text, and Content buttons, as well as the Home and Back buttons, are in the same place.

Hypertext Words

Certain words are often made into hyperlinks in newspaper articles. For example, in the article shown in Figure 4–15, I touched the hyperlinked word "Germany" (see article to the left), and the latest breaking news on this country appeared in a split browser (see screen on right).

INTERNATIONAL GERMAN POLICE ROUT THOUSANDS AT NUCLEAR PRO...

German Police Rout Thousands at Nuclear Protest

By THE ASSOCIATED PRESS

BERLIN (AP) — German police officers cleared a sit-in of thousands of protesters trying to block a train carrying nuclear waste and temporarily detained 1,300 people on Sunday, officials said.

Hundreds of officers started removing protesters from the rails near Dannenberg in northern Germany in the morning, said a police spokesman, Stefan Kühm-Stoltz. Those who resisted were detained at the site for several hours, but all were released by late afternoon.

The police put the number of protesters at 3,500, while organizers said 5,000 people had occupied the tracks, the final stretch for the train. Trucks were to take

Figure 4–15. *Want more information from a newspaper? Use the hyperlink feature.*

As you can see in Figure 4–15, tapping on a hypertext word gives the user access to more information (on the web) about the article. If you want to go back to the original article, just hit the Back button.

The Search Feature

Another terrific feature about the Kindle Fire is that it allows you to look up words as you read. This works for both electronic newspapers and magazines.

Simply select a word by pressing and holding it until you see a blue highlighter. Then swipe along the word to highlight it—and you are provided a definition of the word (see Figure 4–16).

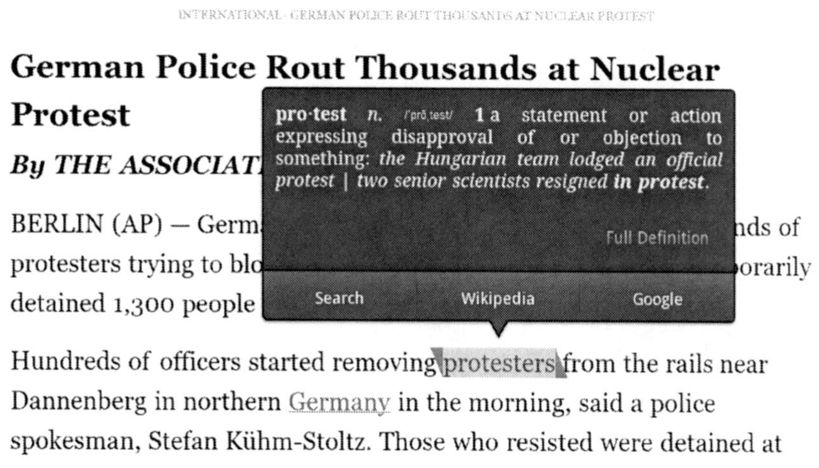
INTERNATIONAL · GERMAN POLICE ROUT THOUSANDS AT NUCLEAR PROTEST
German Police Rout Thousands at Nuclear Protest
By THE ASSOCIAT
BERLIN (AP) — Germ
nds of
protesters trying to blo
orarily
detained 1,300 people
pro·test n. /ˈprōˌtest/ 1 a statement or action expressing disapproval of or objection to something: the Hungarian team lodged an official protest | two senior scientists resigned in protest.
Full Definition
Search
Wikipedia
Google
Hundreds of officers started removing protesters from the rails near Dannenberg in northern Germany in the morning, said a police spokesman, Stefan Kühm-Stoltz. Those who resisted were detained at

Figure 4–16. *Using the word search feature on a Kindle Fire newspaper article*

Tapping on Full Definition at the bottom-right of the pop-up box opens the *New Oxford American Dictionary* in the Books section. This is a free dictionary that comes with the purchase of the Kindle Fire; it allows you to read the full definition of a word. Hit the Back button to return to the article you were reading.

Hitting Search (located at the bottom of the pop-up box) in this mode will search the journal for the highlighted word. It is the same as pressing the Search button and entering in the word. Again, hitting the Back button will return you to your article.

Tapping Wikipedia takes you to the Wikipedia web site in the Kindle Fire's Web browser, which looks up the word in the online encyclopedia. Of course, the reputation of Wikipedia is often questionable, but if you are looking for additional information, you might as well see what Wikipedia has to say.

The Google button performs a Google search of the word, switching your Kindle Fire to web mode so that you can find out even more information from several different choices, as seen in Figure 4–17.

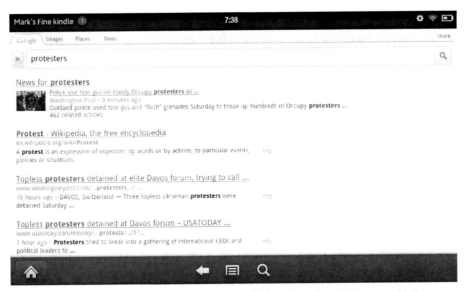

Figure 4–17. *A Google search on the word "protesters", it can branch out into some odd places.*

Working with the Kindle Fire Newsstand

When you purchase magazines and newspapers, your Newsstand shelf should display them (see Figure 4–17). On the Newsstand, you can sort your magazines and newspapers using either By Recent or By Title, which helps you put them in order.

The same rules for organization on the Carousel apply on the Newsstand as well. Pressing and holding a magazine thumbnail gives you the option to Add to Favorites or Remove from Device. A third option, Keep, is also available. The Newsstand is designed to automatically eliminate any issue more than seven months old; but you can choose to "Keep" it if you want. A fourth option, Show Back Issues, is also available, and selecting this will cause all back issues that you have for this newspaper or magazine to appear, as you can see in Figure 4–18.

Figure 4–18. *Your magazine options on the Newsstand*

Journals Available via App

Many journals have tablet versions that are available for free, provided you are a subscriber to the print edition.

In the Apps category, you can find a lot of popular magazine apps by entering "magazines" in the search engine (see Figure 14–18).

Figure 4–19. *Many magazines for the Kindle Fire are available in app form.*

As you can see in Figure 4–19, many applications are available for free. One of these magazines is *Wired*, a science and technology magazine available for subscription by touching the Free button, which takes you to a screen where you can formally subscribe (see Figure 4–20).

Figure 4–20. *Subscribing to* Wired Magazine *on the Kindle Fire*

Once you have subscribed, you can access the application/magazine. But, there is an entirely different set of rules for navigation.

For example, the *Parents* magazine/app for the Kindle Fire has an index at the front that opens a menu to access the Cover, Age Guide, Playbook, Page Viewer, Store, and Library. The Page Viewer feature is shown in Figure 4–21.

Figure 4–21. *The* Parents *magazine app for the Kindle Fire*

You will notice that in Figure 4–21, The Parents.com Poll has a 45% marked on "Street Smart". This was not something that appears on all copies of the magazine, but something that appeared when I touched "Street Smart". I have no idea if I just voted on this, and my vote is a part of this 45%. The entire Parents magazine/application is as interactive as this.

Managing Your Subscriptions Online

You might be picking up a lot of magazines and newspapers with a free trial, but this could lead to unwanted payments if you forget to unsubscribe. Fortunately, Amazon makes it easy for you to manage all your subscriptions in one place. Just go to www.amazon.com/manageyourkindlesubscriptions and log into your account. You will find yourself on a page that looks like Figure 4–22.

Your Account   Manage Your Kindle

Figure 4–22. *My Manage Your Kindle Account page on Amazon*

You can see that I have two subscriptions, one for *W Magazine* and the other for *The New York Times*. The Actions button, which appears on the far right of each subscription setting, provides several features in its menu. One such feature is Deliver Past Issue, which allows a specific issue to be sent directly to a Kindle device (see Figure 4–23).

Figure 4–23. *Delivering a past issue to your Kindle Fire*

Another way to get a past issue is to use a USB to micro-USB connection, an accessory discussed in Chapter 3 (see Figure 4–24). This will allow you to transfer a magazine copy to your computer, provided that USB to micro-USB cable is connected.

Figure 4–24. *Downloading a magazine issue via USB*

You can also cancel a subscription from the Actions menu. Then, all you need to do is simply fill out the window like the one shown in Figure 4–25.

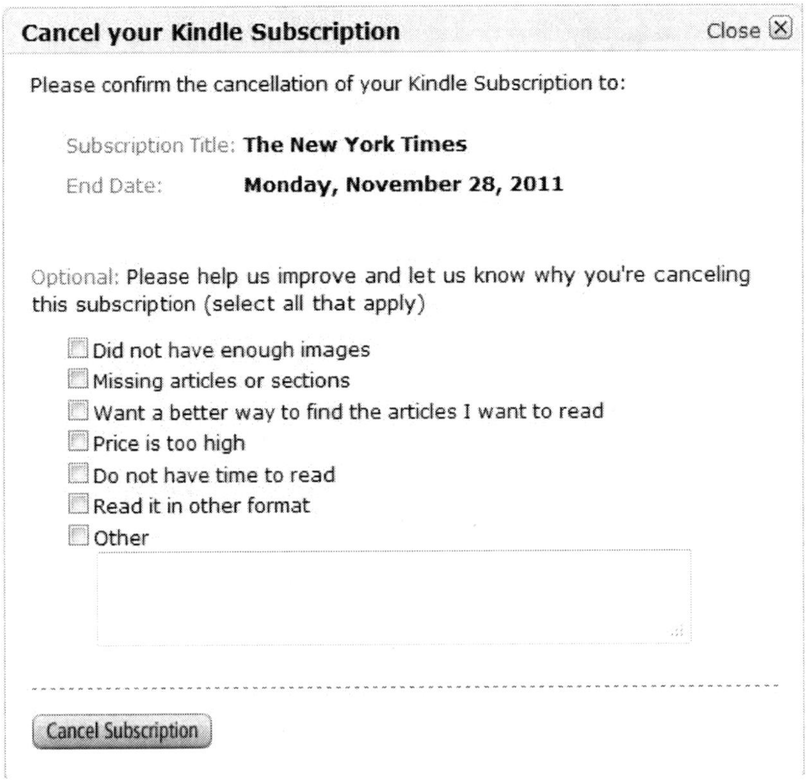

Figure 4–25. *Canceling a subscription to a magazine or newspaper*

You can also set up payment plans and other options under the Actions button menu.

Summary

The Kindle Fire Newsstand comes with no magazines or newspapers included, but it is very easy to purchase them. All that is required is an internet connection and shopping at Amazon's store, which can be accomplished from the Kindle Fire device or online from a separate computer. Several magazines and newspapers are available for a free trial, so that you can try them before you invest your money.

Reading a magazine or newspaper on the Kindle Fire is as simple as swiping your finger. You can read in either portrait or landscape format. The control buttons give instant access to a Table of Contents, and magazine pages can be viewed in Page View or Text View format. The Page View looks more like the actual printed magazine and the Text button allows the user further control of the Font Styles and the Typeface.

Another feature for magazines and newspapers is hypertext, which is useful for looking up words or phrases in the dictionary or online through Google or Wikipedia.

Some magazines are available as applications. This allows a lot more interesting interactivity when it comes to reading the magazine itself. A lot of magazine/applications (like Parents, for instance) take full advantage of the Kindle Fire's touchscreen and are more of an ever-changing application than a static printed page.

Kindle Fire users can also manage their subscriptions online. It is also possible to purchase back issues online, and even transfer the issues to your computer.

In short, you will find that you will need to reevaluate how you do your subscriptions after you use the Kindle Fire Newsstand. With any luck, you can digitize your magazine and newspaper world, and save some money in the process.

Chapter 5

Books

Considering that the sole purpose of the original Kindle was to read electronic books, you are going to need to know how to purchase and read books on the Amazon Kindle Fire. This chapter will show you how to find and purchase books on the Kindle Fire, and what you can do with them once you have them. It will even cover a bit about Audible and how to purchase audiobooks.

If you choose the Books option on the homsescreen, it will open up a shelf and you can see, by default, the Oxford American Dictionary is one of the books (I have ordered some books of my own). As far as I know, the shelf can literally go on forever, just like in the Newsstand and homescreen (see Figure 5–1, left). In fact, the shelf space is pretty much infinite thanks to the Cloud capability, it is the Device that will limit you.

Figure 5–1. *The Kindle Books category, and the Book Store.*

The Kindle Fire Bookstore

As you can see on Figure 5–1 (right), the Store set up is pretty obvious and quite similar to that of the Newsstand. On the top is the Search engine for the bookstore, so you can type in and look for whatever book you are looking for by Title, Subject, and Author.

Below the Recommended section and the Search engine, and you can use that to find whatever book you are looking for, if it is available in Kindle form.

You will find categories to the left, which include Top 100 Paid, Children's Picture Books, Best Fiction of the year, New and Noteworthy, Kindle Singles, and Top 100 Free.

On the right, you will find other categories, and before I go into detail on them, I will talk about a button that appears in every category known as Refine.

The Refine Button

Within Kindle Singles, you will notice a button in the upper right hand corner that says "Refine" (see Figure 5–2).

Figure 5–2. *The Refine button, on Kindle Singles, a very useful button when looking for a specific type of book.*

Refine is a helpful button to help you find what you are looking for, and if you press it, you will find that you can choose "Sort By" in five categories:

- Bestselling
- Price: Low to High
- Price: High to Low
- Avg. Customer Review
- Publication Date

As for Refine's Category, it is only set for Kindle Singles, but for other genres of books, it will sort by other factors.

You can also sort by Customer Reviews from one star to four stars and up.

Categories of Book Browsing

For Browse Books, you will find a way to select all kinds of subjects with just a touch, including:

- Kindle eBooks
- Fiction
- Nonfiction
- Advice & How-to
- Arts & Entertainment
- Biographies & Memoirs
- Business & Investing
- Children's eBooks
- Comics & Graphic Novels
- Computers & Internet
- Cooking, Food, & Wine
- Fantasy
- History
- Humor
- Lifestyle & Home
- Literary Fiction
- Mystery & Thrillers
- Parenting & Families
- Politics & Current Events
- Reference
- Religion & Spirituality
- Romance
- Science
- Science Fiction
- Sports
- Travel

As for Kindle Singles, these are, in Amazon's own words, "compelling ideas expressed at their natural length". They are essays and short stories, rather than a full-length book or novel. Several of these are published independently, and although there are few to select from at this writing, I have no doubt that there will be a lot more in the years to come.

Visit the Newstand will take you back to the Newsstand that we discussed in the last chapter.

Editor's Picks is chosen by Amazon, but they don't seem to have their names listed. On this section is both fiction and non-fiction books, as well as Kindle Singles.

Kindle Owner's Lending Library is for Amazon Prime members, and it allows its members to choose from thousands of books to borrow for free which include over 100 current and former New York Times bestsellers. One book per month can be checked out, with no due dates. (You will find that Amazon will "take the book back", and I found that my monthly book had disappeared from my shelf after I left Amazon Prime membership.)

NY Best Sellers sorts out the books on the bestseller list. I have checked out what it defaults to compared to what is on the actual New York Times Bestseller list, and it isn't always a perfect match. If you want to buy the latest book on the bestseller list, you should probably double check by going to http://www.nytimes.com/best-sellers-books/overview.html.

Children's Picture Books and Comic Books actually work well for the Kindle Fire, and I will discuss them a little later. Right now, let's talk about simply buying a book on the Kindle Fire.

Buying a book for the Kindle Fire

Selecting a book to buy on the Kindle Fire is just like buying a magazine or newspaper on the Newsstand, with a few differences.

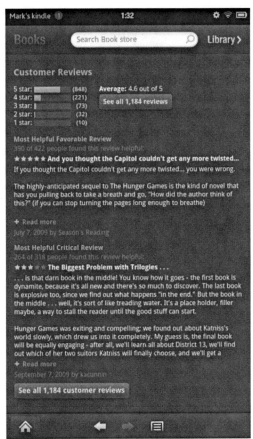

Figure 5–3. *A book entry for the Kindle Fire Books.*

As you can see by Figure 5–3, the entry for each book has the Title, Author, Description, Recommendations, but book entries have Customer Reviews ranging from one to five stars. I don't really read these much, but if you are interested, you can check them out. As you might have guessed, this particular book, *Catching Fire*, has quite a lot of reviews at over one thousand.

Buying a book is as simple as the ease of touching of button, but unlike subscribing to a magazine, you have the option of borrowing it for free. As stated before, this is limited on Amazon Prime to once per month.

There is also the option of getting a Sample. This is a few pages of the book for free that you can read just so you can decide whether or not you want to buy the book yourself.

Usually, it is the first chapter of a book, but only the first few pages for the singles. These books will appear on your bookshelf and the homescreen with an obvious label of "Sample" written on them.

Reading a book on the Kindle Fire

Reading a book is as simple as tapping the book on the shelf, or on the Carousel or Favorities at the homescreen. Once the book is open, it is easy to access the commands below by touching the bottom of the screen.

Finger swipes to the left and right are good for forward and backward page-turning, respectively. One of things you will notice about reading an e-book is that page numbers are not like that of a printed book. On the Kindle Fire, the page is designated by a "Location", and will have a percentage of your completion right by it, as seen in Figure 5–4.

"So you really hate them?"

"Yes. But they're extraordinary. Really," I say. And they are. But I don't want to look at them anymore. "Want to see my talent? Cinna did a great job on it."

Peeta laughs. "Later." The train lurches forward, and I can see the land moving past us through the window. "Come on, we're almost to District Eleven. Let's go take a look at it."

We go down to the last car on the train. There are chairs and couches to sit on, but what's wonderful is that the back windows retract

Figure 5–4. *The control options for a book on the Kindle Fire.*

You will note the buttons on the bottom, and they are the same as the ones at the Newsstand. The text button marked "Aa" is exactly the same as I described in the last chapter. What is really different is what the Contents button can do, but I will describe that later. For now, I want to discuss the bookmarking feature.

Bookmarking a Page

Bookmarking a Page on the Kindle Fire is about the easiest thing to learn. For the sake of being thorough, I will briefly say that it is as simple touching the bookmark in the right hand corner, which is visible when the other menu options are visible. You can see it as a clear bookmark in Figure 5–4. When you are ready to bookmark your page, just touch bookmark tab. Touching bookmark again will remove it. I'll discuss how to view your bookmarks in the Contents section below.

Texting Highlight

Like the Newsstand, you can highlight words or words, but with different options.

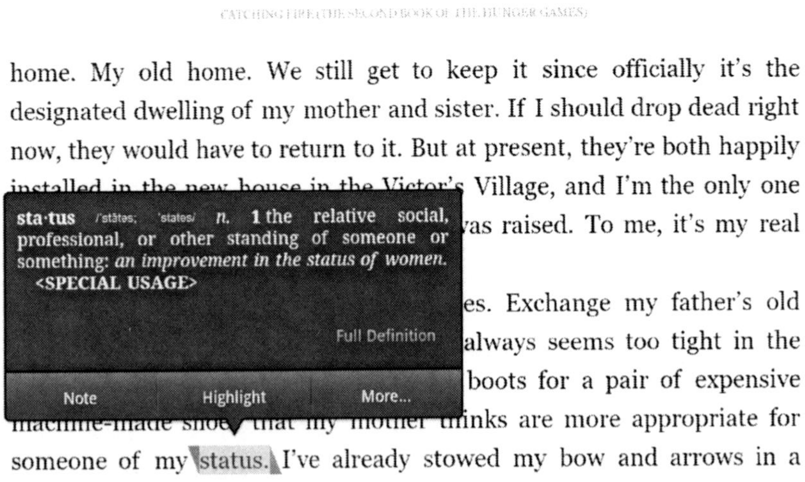

Figure 5–5. *What happens when you highlight a word or words on a Kindle Fire ebook. You have options.*

Touching the "Full Definition" word will send you to another book: the *New Oxford American Dictionary*. Here you can see a truly full definition of the word. This is just like in the Newsstand feature, and you can hit Back when you want to go back.

The Notes feature is for when you want to make a special note about a certain part in the book. This is especially handy when you are using the Kindle Fire as a substitute for traditional printed textbooks. Think about anything that you wrote in the margins so you would remember for later. All that is required is pressing on "Note" and typing it in on the keyboard, as seen in Figure 5–6. Once it is typed in, go ahead and hit "Save". You will see a small folded piece of paper by the section, and the Contents Menu, which I will describe later, will help you access your notes.

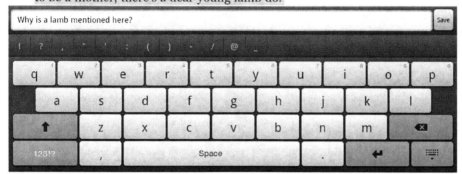

Figure 5–6. *Making a note on an ebook.*

As for the Highlight, that is exactly what it looks like. Just think of all the times you used a highlighter to make certain passages stand out. Yellow is the only color available, at least for this version of the Kindle Fire.

The other option is the More… feature, and this gives three choices:

- Search in Book
- Search Wikipedia
- Search Google

The Search in Book allows you to search the word or words, just like you would have entered it into the Search Engine. Search Wikipedia and Search Google are just like in Newsstand, and will jump you to the Web to look for your word or words. Again, hitting the back button will send you back to the book.

The Contents Button

Hitting the Contents Button on an eBook produces a very different effect than on the Newsstand, as you can see in Figure 5–7.

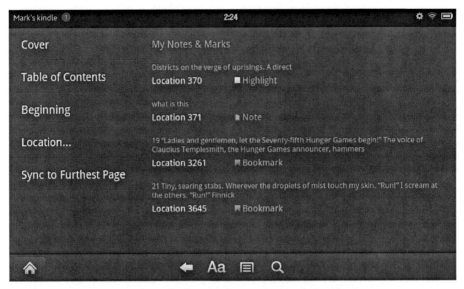

Figure 5–7. *What you will see after hitting the "Contents" button for an ebook.*

On the right you will see the "My Notes & Marks" section. This is where you can see your Notes, Highlights, and Bookmarks that I discussed earlier in this chapter. If you press and hold the Highlights and Bookmarks, you will be given the choice of Viewing them or Deleting them. If you press and hold the Notes, you can also view, delete, and edit them.

As for the options on the left side, they include:

- Cover: Touching this will take you to the cover of the book.

- Table of Contents: This opens up the Table of Contents, which is very useful on an ebook, as every chapter number is a link. Touching a chapter will send you to the beginning of the chapter, instantly.

- Beginning: This will start you off at the beginning of the book.

- Location: Pressing this will open up a numerical keyboard function, and you can enter in the location (the digital version of a page number) that you want.

- Sync to Furthest Page: This button will take you as far along in the book as you have progressed so far. If you have finished the book, and started again, this does reprogram itself.

You will find that selecting text is quite limited on Children's books as well as the comic books on the Kindle Fire.

Children's Books on the Kindle Fire

One great advantage of having full color on the Kindle Fire is that children's books no longer have to look monochrome anymore. This comes in handy for when taking a long trip, and you have kids in the backseat. One book can only last them so long, but the Kindle Fire can hold many, even without the Cloud Storage.

Children's books on the Kindle Fire often have a special feature. By double tapping on the text, it grows in size. See Figure 5–8 for a demonstration on Eric Carle's *Brown Bear, Brown Bear, What do you see?*

Figure 5–8. *What happens when you double-tap the text on a children's book on the Kindle Fire.*

As someone who is a parent myself, I want to give all parents a piece of advice. The Kindle Fire is an excellent tool for buying and downloading children's books, but this can easily be abused, especially by a child. For this reason, I would suggest locking your account so only you can use it, unless you want to see massive bills from Amazon. That, and don't allow your child to use a Kindle Fire unsupervised.

Comic Books on the Kindle Fire

Like Children's Books, Comic Books have been put in full color. I found that the comic books can only be read in portrait view, and the seven-inch diagonal isn't the same size as a regular printed comic book.

Fortunately, the user has the option of magnifying a single comic-book panel, which is similar to double-tapping the text on a children's book. In this case, double-tapping a single panel will bring it out, as you can see in Figure 5–9 with the classic graphic novel *Watchmen*.

Figure 5–9. *Reading a graphic novel on the Kindle Fire. This is what double-tapping will do.*

It should be noted that Amazon has made an exclusive deal with comic book companies to put out digital versions of their graphic novel collections, some for the first time. You will notice that most of your choices will be limited to DC and Vertigo comics. If you are looking for issues by Marvel or other comic book companies, you might be able to find the issues you are looking for on an application known as Comics by ComiXology. Just run a search on the App store for Comics, and then you can purchase your Marvel comics individually. Comics is also a good tool for when you are looking for one single issue of a graphic novel, rather than the entire collected set.

Managing your Books online

In the last chapter, I discussed how you can manage your subscriptions online at `http://www.amazon.com/manageyourkindlesubscriptions`, and you can also manage books from here as well.

If you click on the Books link on the left side, as seen in Figure 5–10, you can see that all the books on your shelf are there, and you can do many things with them from here.

Figure 5–10. *Managing your books on Kindle's subscription manager, online.*

You will notice that after every book is "Actions…", clicking on this unlocks a number of options. For example, you can download and transfer via USB. You can also delete the book from the library. If you have a book on loan from the Kindle Lending Library on Amazon.com, you can return it here.

You will discover that one of the actions is "Read Now". This will immediately open up the work in the Cloud Reader on your computer, as seen in Figure 5–11.

Figure 5–11. *The Cloud Reader on your computer.*

You will notice that the Cloud Reader has several options on its top menu bar. Clicking on "Library" will open up the option of reading all your books on your computer's browser. You will be able to see them all like in Figure 5–12.

Figure 5–12. *All the books available to read on the Cloud Reader, as seen by a browser.*

The rest of the menu is devoted to other commands, the open book will immediately take you to the Cover, Table of Contents, Beginning, (specific) Location, and Book Extras.

The Aa is a way of adjusting the font fact, which is good for both Font Size, Margins, and Color Mode.

The Bookmark is for marking a bookmark, and the symbol next to it is how to access the bookmark.

The last symbol is the "Sync to Furthest Page Read", which will take you as far as you have read in your particular book.

By the way, if a book is removed from you, the notes and the furthest page read are saved in case you wish to borrow it again or purchase it.

Using Audible for listening to e-books

Earlier versions of the Kindle had a text-to-speech feature, but unfortunately, this feature is not available on the e-books bought at the Amazon e-book store. However, there is an application known as Audible which is capable of providing audiobooks for many books. Audible was acquired by Amazon in 2008, and it works slightly different than the Books category.

If you go to the Apps category, you can access the application from there, which comes with the Kindle Fire by default. If you need help with that, go to Chapter 9 on Apps for further guidance. The opening screen looks like Figure 5–13.

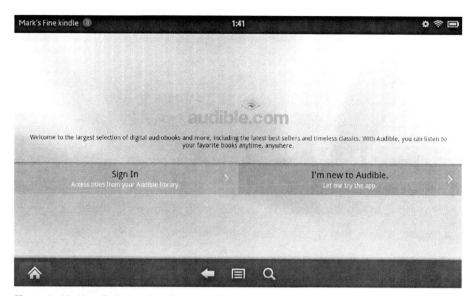

Figure 5–13. *Your first step of getting on audible.com.*

You will then see a confirmation of your marketplace, which will be either one of the three. When you select it, I found that the screen faded to black. I found I had to open the application again, and I saw a screen that looked like Figure 5–14.

Figure 5–14. *The main menu page of audible.com.*

You can see that you have access to several audiobooks, and some of them include some major bestsellers including Steig Larsson's *The Girl Who Kicked a Hornet's Nest* and classics like Ernest Hemingway's *A Farewell to Arms*. Unfortunately, they are all excerpts, and the choices are very limited.

You will note that you can sort them by

- Recent, putting the most recently published titles first.

- Title, which sorts the audiobooks in alphabetical order by title.

- Author, which sorts the audiobooks in alphabetical order by author.

- Length, which sorts the audiobooks by length (of time not pages) with the smallest being the first.

Touching and holding that is not downloaded will reveal two options:

- Download, which will begin downloading of the book right away.

- Read Summary, which will open up a window for a summary of the book.

Touching and holding a book that is downloaded will reveal these three choices:

- Play, which will start the audio book.

- Remove from device, which will take the audiobook off the Kindle Fire.

- Read summary, which does exactly what it does before the book is downloaded.

The down arrow that you see at the end of the entry is the button to push for downloading an audiobook. This will become a play arrow as it downloads, and pushing the arrow will go to a screen that you see in Figure 5–15. By the way, you have the option of listening to the audiobook while it is downloading. When the audio book is downloaded, there will not be an arrow at the end, but the time remaining. Touch it to reveal a screen like Figure 5.

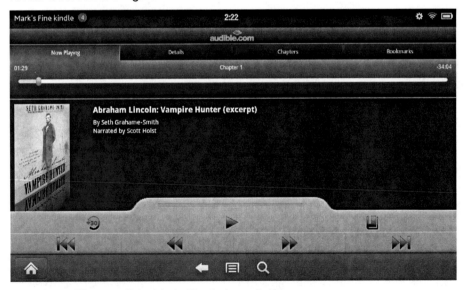

Figure 5–15. *What an audiobook looks like playing on Audible.*

You can see the list of choices, so I will start with the menu bar on top.

- Now Playing, this shows what is playing, with the cover, author, and narrator. Touching the cover of the book will enlarge the cover art.

- Details. This has more information on the audiobook, which includes the Length, File Size, Publisher, and Format.

- Chapters. This allows you to select a specific chapter of the work with just a touch.

- Bookmarks: Audible allows you to bookmark a section, and you can even leave a comment on your bookmark. I will explain how to do it later, but this is how you access them. Touching a bookmark will take you to the spot in the book.

You will notice that there is a bar below the chapter designation, and you can see the time markers. Adjusting the bar can be done quickly or slowly, all that is required is sliding your finger up and down to adjust the scrubbing speed.

As for the controls below, you will notice several:

- Back 30 seconds, helpful for when you just missed that last part, or in case you can't remember where you left off.

- Play/Pause, for resuming or stopping reading. It will save it after you pause, so there isn't a need to bookmark.

- Bookmark, if you select this, you will be given two options. The last is close, and the other is "Add Notes". If you click it, you can leave a note on the section. You can then access it again on the Bookmarks section in the top menu.

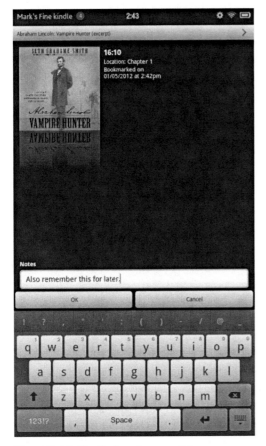
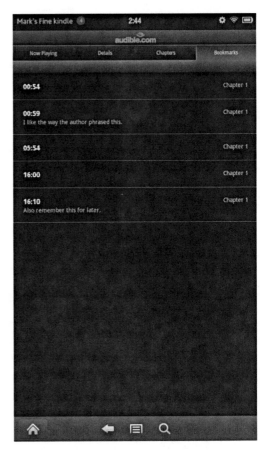

Figure 5–16. *The Bookmarks on audible.com.*

The last four controls are only accessible when the tap above the Play/Pause is swiped. These are the controls, from left to right.

- Chapter Rewind: Allows you to go to the last chapter.
- Rewind: Depening on how many times you touch this, this rewind button will go back 2x, 4x, or 8x.
- Fast Forward: This will also fast forward it, with the same speeds of 2x, 4x, or 8x.
- Chapter Forward: This will advance to the next chapter.

As for the bottom menu, the back button works as you would expect it to. It does have a Contents Menu that is capable of six options:

Share: This allows you to share via Facebook, e-mail, or other related apps. You can tell others about what you are reading on audible, and will even give a link to audiobook.

Sleep: This will turn the audiobook off after a certain amount of time.

Button-Free: This creates an interface that you can see in Figure 5–17.

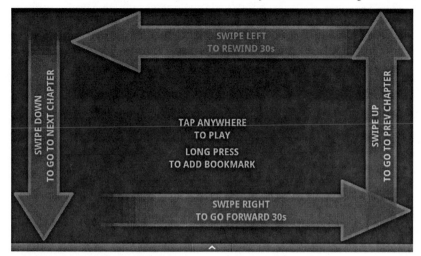

Figure 5–17. *The Button-free Interface.*

My Library: Take you back to the original screen where are all the books are.

Narrator Speed: In case you want to change the speed of the book being read, this is how it is done. This is actually quite helpful for when you want it read faster when you are in a hurry, or slower, in case you want to take more in.

Quit. Takes you out of the application altogether.

Setting up an Audible account

You will notice in the upper right corner of the homescreen a button that allows you to create an account. Pressing it will allow you to go straight to a screen where you can use your Amazon account to create an Audible account (see Figure 5–18).

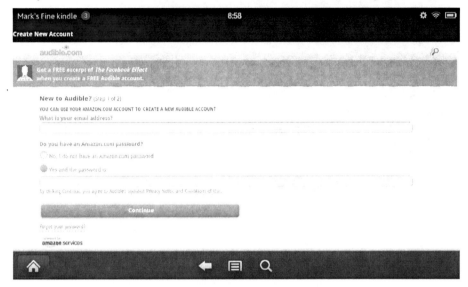

Figure 5–18. *Setting up an Audible account with an Amazon account.*

From there, it is pretty easy to start up the application, and you can log in to your account. Access to the market is done with the shopping cart in the corner.

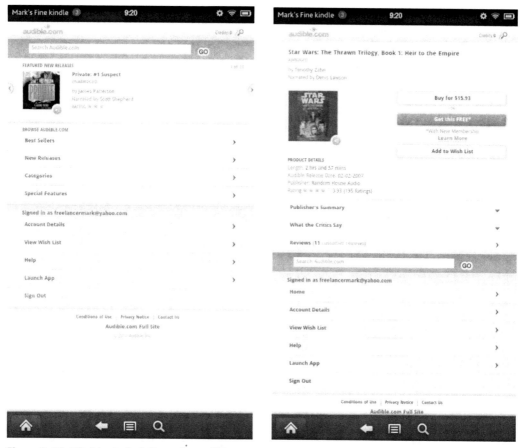

Figure 5–19. *What books look like on the audible.com site.*

Here on the market you can see a number of choices, including the Content Menu:

- Shop. This will take you to the Shop where you can buy books.

- News. This brings up some news features.

- Stats. Audible likes to keep its readers awarded.

- Search. This will search only the library for the audiobook that you are looking for.

- Settings. This includes a lot of set up things like:

  - About this Application, allowing you to share the App, and access to Legal Notices.

  - General Settings, and will allow you to disable auto lock, and the possibility of shopping in the Browser.

  - Playback Settings which allows you to adjust the back button, forward button, and seamless multipart play.

- Download Settings allows for Standard Quality and High Quality downloading formats.

- Headset settings. For those who are listening to the audiobook with some sort of headphone, this will enable some interest.

- Help and Support. A way of getting sending a message to Audible when there is a problem.

- Sign out. A way of signing out of the application.

- Quit. Exits the application.

Summary

Since Amazon has made a name in e-books with many versions of the Kindle, the Kindle Fire has been made very simple to find what e-book you are looking for with the "Refine" button. They have also made it very easy to purchase and download the book, or even get a loaner book for Amazon Prime members.

Reading a book on the Kindle Fire is very efficient, as it comes with the Notes, Highlights, and Bookmark feature. Also included is the Contents feature which will take you immediately to the location of choice without any flipping.

In addition to the texting highlight, which helps the reader learn more about their book content, the Kindle Fire is excellent for reading both children's books and comic books. In each case, double tapping increases the size of certain content, making it easier to read.

Like the Newsstand, Books can be managed online with the "Manage My Subscriptions". This comes in especially handy for quickly deleting books, or moving them to other memory sources.

In addition to getting textual books for reading, the Kindle Fire has access to audible.com, an application that allows you to purchase audio books for listening. Managing these is different than the traditional books, so make certain that you know how to use them.

You will find that you will be able to save a lot of money and be able to read more books in Amazon's e-book format. I certainly recommend looking into it, especially if you are the type who devours many books.

Chapter 6

Music

It is hard to believe that the way that music is distributed and sold has changed so much in so little time. Thanks to the internet and MP3 players, CDs are almost a dead format. Every once in a while, I wonder how long it will be before all music is digital.

The Kindle Fire is prepared for this era with its Music feature. Like iTunes for the iPod, the Kindle Fire has its own Music store so that you can buy the music that you want to hear, and put it in a playlist so that you can hear it in whatever order that you desire.

You can listen to your personalized playlists while you are doing other tasks on Kindle Fire, like reading a journal from the Newsstand, reading an e-book, surfing the web, or running an app. As long as what you are doing in the foreground requires minimal audio, you can have your music playing in the background.

Some of you have massive playlists on your computer, and they can be put on the Kindle Fire along with new tunes. Any music file that is played on the Kindle Fire, whether on the cloud or on the device itself, can be listened to on an internet-connected computer as well.

Getting Music from Your Computer to the Kindle Fire

The Kindle Fire comes with no default files, so you will have to purchase or upload music. The Music default screen looks like that shown in Figure 6–1.

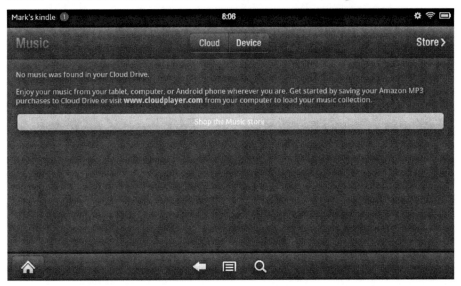

Figure 6–1. *The default Music screen*

You can access the Music store with the Store button in the top right corner. The Cloud/Device selection is also available. Cloud is for the music that will be on the Cloud Player; Device is for the tunes that will only play on the device. Sure, you have the option of playing all your music on the cloud, but if you are going to be in an area where there isn't any Wi-Fi, then you will want to have your music on the device.

Before I start talking about how to get music on the device, let's talk about getting music on the cloud. Tapping the big yellow Shop the Music store bar takes you straight to the Amazon Music store. Or, you can go to `www.cloudplayer.com` on a separate computer for music selections.

Amazon's Cloud Player is integrated with the company's MP3 store so that music can be stored on your Cloud Drive account. You need to go to the Cloud Player web site and use your Amazon password to get in (see Figure 6–2).

Figure 6–2. *Opening Amazon's Cloud Drive on a separate PC*

Click Upload your music; you will get a prompt to download the Amazon Cloud Player to your computer. Do this, keeping in mind that the Kindle Fire can only play MP3 and AAC files, so the Cloud Player will only look for these specific files.

Next, you see an application install window, as shown in Figure 6–3.

Figure 6–3. *Downloading the Cloud Player onto your computer*

As you can see in the description, the MP3 Uploader is essentially asking for permission to upload your music library, including playlists, to the Kindle Fire cloud storage area. This includes iTunes and Windows Media Player music libraries—unless these audio files are limited use, as with DRM (Digital Rights Management) technology. This makes it very easy for you to get your music onto your Kindle as quickly as possible.

Installing Adobe AIR 3.1 is required. Before installing, the program asks you to accept a user license agreement, as shown in Figure 6–4.

Figure 6–4. *Adobe AIR user license agreement*

Once you have agreed, the program starts to download. When it's done, you should see a window like the one shown in Figure 6–5.

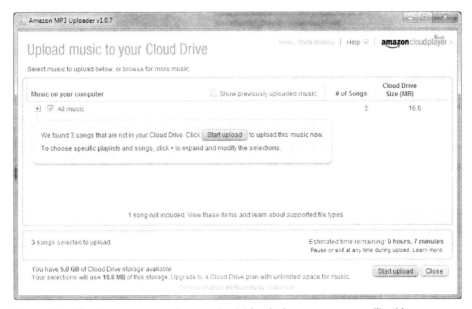

Figure 6–5. *After the program searches your hard drive, it gives you a message like this one.*

This window lets you know which songs are about to be downloaded. Hit Start Upload, and the music that is detected will begin to upload.

At one point, you will be asked to save to either the cloud or the device. Select the one that you want. Keep in mind that the cloud has a lot more memory, so you should go with that as much as you can. Granted, you will need to be connected to the internet to access the cloud, so you might want to put the music on your device if you plan to listen to music on a long trip without an internet connection.

Eventually, you should be able to open your Amazon Kindle and find all your MP3 files as you open Music on the Home screen. Your songs will be ready to play, provided that you switch to the Cloud option, or whatever option you chose to save it on.

Your Music screen should now look something like Figure 6–6.

Figure 6–6. *The Music feature after songs have been downloaded*

Figure 6–6 shows that songs are sorted by Artists, Albums, Songs, and Playlists.

One of the great things about playing audio files on the Kindle Fire is that they play in the background, so you can hear music while you read if you want. As soon your tunes are playing, you can go to the Home screen and select whatever other category that you wish to run.

To have your music play in the background, tap on the Settings icon (the cog) in the top right corner. You should then see a screen like the one shown in Figure 6–7.

Figure 6–7. *An example of what you see when playing a track in the background*

You also have the option of pausing the audio file, as well as advancing or rewinding it one track on the playlist.

Creating a Playlist

Sometimes it is simply easier to group songs together rather than repeatedly selecting them from the giant group of songs that you will eventually have after several downloads. To create a playlist, you need to do the following:

1. Select Create New Playlist, as seen in Figure 6–6.

2. Type in the name that you want for your playlist (see Figure 6–8).

Figure 6–8. *Naming your playlist*

3. Select the songs that you want (see Figure 6–9). If are having trouble finding a song, use the search engine to find it.

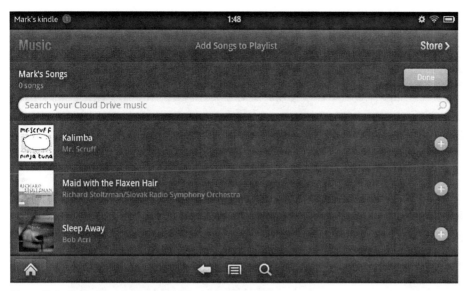

Figure 6–9. *To make a playlist, select the songs you want*

4. Tap Done to complete your playlist.

Editing a Playlist

Once you have a playlist, you can edit it. All that is required is to tap the Edit button in the top right corner, as seen in Figure 6–10.

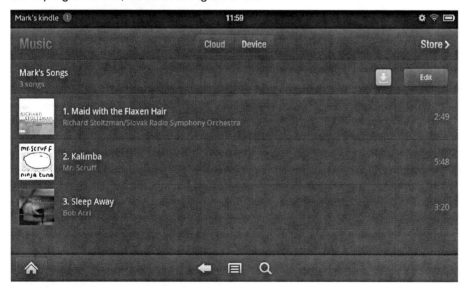

Figure 6–10. *Editing an existing playlist*

The playlist in Figure 6–11 is called "Mark's Songs." Notice that there is a minus sign button after each song; tapping it erases the song from the playlist.

Figure 6–11. *Options for editing a playlist on the Kindle Fire*

If you tap the Add button, you are lead to a screen that shows all your songs in a scrollable list (see Figure 6–12). If you are having a hard time locating a particular song, you can try the search engine.

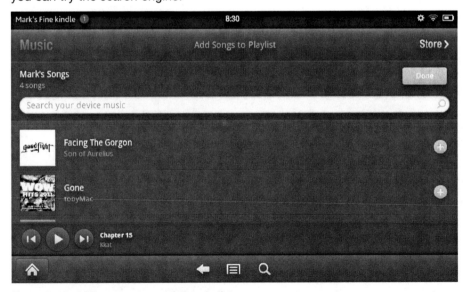

Figure 6–12. *Adding songs to an existing playlist*

Tapping the plus sign button next to song title adds it to the playlist. Hitting Done ensures that the songs remain on the playlist and exit you from Edit Playlist mode.

Although I have tried, I have not figured out a way to change the order of songs on an existing playlist.

The Amazon Music Store

You can always search the Amazon Music store for new music. The store format is very similar to the Newsstand and Books stores.

The search engine is prominently featured top center, as shown in Figure 6–13. You will get a lot of use out of it if you know the name of the song or artist that you are looking for.

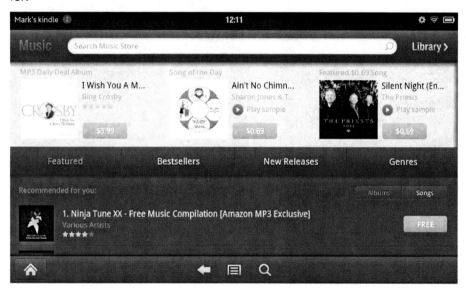

Figure 6–13. *The Music store on the Kindle Fire*

The Music store is definitely made for browsing. The top bar has categories like MPE Daily Deal Album, Song of the Day, and others. Below this are Featured, Bestsellers, New Releases, and Genres.

The Featured area is the category that the Music store defaults to. It recommends music for you to purchase. As you can see in Figure 6–13, its top selection is a free album. I think this was selected for me personally because I have been perusing free music.

Bestsellers is all about the top hits. There are two options: Albums and Songs (see Figure 6–14, left).

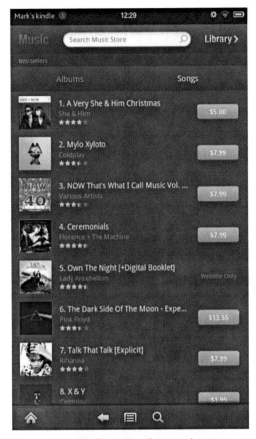

Figure 6–14. *The Bestseller albums and songs*

Touching an album opens a list of its songs. You can choose to buy the entire album or just buy a song or songs from it. This is very helpful when you really only want one or a few select songs song from an album.

If you want to hear a 30-second sample of a song before you buy it, tap the Play button to the left of the song number/name (see Figure 6–14, right). These 30 seconds are not necessarily the first 30 seconds; the sample may play from the middle of the song.

The New Releases category essentially has the same format as Bestsellers, except the music here is newly released. You can also sample the albums' songs.

In the Genres section, you can really browse for your favorite types of music. The basic list includes:

- Alternative Rock
- Blues
- Broadway & Vocalists
- Children's Music

- Christian & Gospel
- Classic Rock
- Classical
- Country
- Dance & DJ
- Folk
- Hard Rock & Metal
- International
- Jazz
- Latin Music
- Miscellaneous
- New Age
- Opera & Vocal
- Pop
- R&B
- Rap & Hip-Hop
- Rock
- Soundtracks

This is really just the beginning because each genre has sub-genres. Just think of it as going through a record store.

Purchcasing a Song or Album

When you purchase an album or song on the Amazon Music store, it downloads instantly—like an e-journal or e-book. You choose where it goes from there. You are given a choice to put the song/album on the Cloud Player or your device.

Like purchasing digital journals or books on the Kindle Fire, you can manage your music purchases online. If you go to www.amazon.com/manageyourkindlesubscriptions, you find Manage Your MP3s at the bottom of the navigation menu (see Figure 6–15).

Figure 6–15. *Managing your subscriptions also gives you access to your MP3s.*

This takes you directly to your Cloud Player, where you can create and edit playlists (as well as many other things) on your Kindle Fire (see Figure 6–16).

Figure 6–16. *The Amazon Cloud Player, a very useful tool*

Downloading a Song from the Cloud Player

In Figure 6–16, "Party Rock Anthem" by Lmfao is checked. I bought this particular song from the Amazon Music store and I can play it on the Amazon Cloud Player from any computer connected to the internet.

I also have the option of downloading the song to my computer's iTunes or Windows Media Player. All that is required is to select it in the checkbox and click Download. This opens the option to download the Amazon MP3 Downloader, as shown in Figure 6–17.

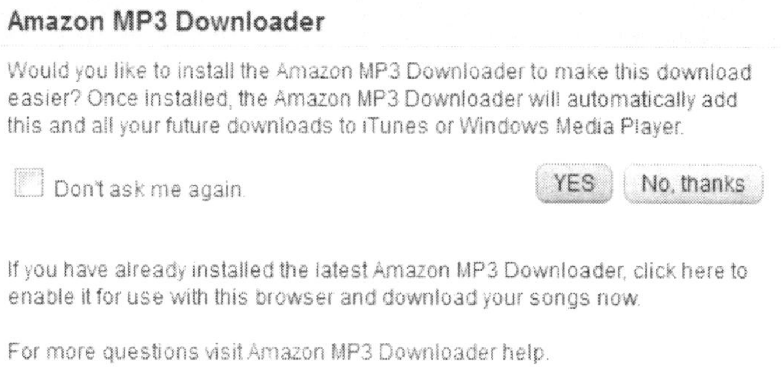

Amazon MP3 Downloader

Would you like to install the Amazon MP3 Downloader to make this download easier? Once installed, the Amazon MP3 Downloader will automatically add this and all your future downloads to iTunes or Windows Media Player.

☐ Don't ask me again.   YES   No, thanks

If you have already installed the latest Amazon MP3 Downloader, click here to enable it for use with this browser and download your songs now.

For more questions visit Amazon MP3 Downloader help.

Figure 6–17. *An offer to download the Amazon MP3 Downloader*

If you do not have this downloader, simply click the YES button and it will automatically download. If you already have the Amazon MP3 Downloader, click the "click here" link. You will be directed to a window similar to the one shown in Figure 6–18.

Figure 6–18. *Downloading a music file from the Kindle Fire to your computer*

I found that choosing Save File puts the music file in the My Downloads folder. I could access the song from there, opening it with the Windows Media Player.

Uploading an Audio File from a Third-Party Source

I'm certain that some of you want music or some other type of audio file that is not available on iTunes or other music sources. For example, I have a friend who has written a story and he has an audio version of the chapters available for downloading that you can find at www.equestriadaily.com/2011/04/story-fallout-equestria.html, as shown in Figure 6–19.

Audio Book Downloads

Introduction
Prologue
Chapter 1
Chapter 2
Chapter 3
Chapter 4
Chapter 5
Chapter 6
Chapter 7
Chapter 8
Chapter 9
Chapter 10
Chapter 11
Chapter 12
Chapter 13
Chapter 14
Chapter 15
Chapter 16
Chapter 17
Chapter 18
Chapter 19
Epilogue

Figure 6–19. *Audio books at Equestria Daily, one of many sites with free audio to download*

If you click one of the chapters, you are directed to a page where you can download it (see Figure 6–20, left). The file may take a while to download, but it should appear in your Downloads folder (see Figure 6–20, right).

Figure 6–20. *Downloading an audio file from a third-party source to the Kindle Fire*

From there, you can upload your file to your Kindle. Open Manageyoursubscriptions and click the Upload Your Music button. Next, you see a window similar to the one shown in Figure 6–21.

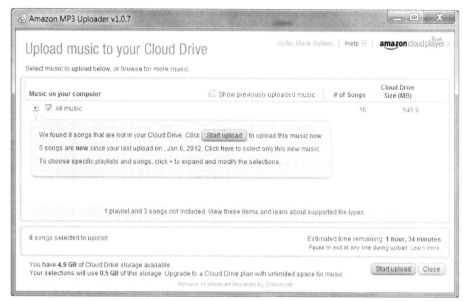

Figure 6–21. *Selecting music to upload to the Cloud Drive*

My computer found eight songs to upload onto the Cloud Drive. If I don't want all of them, I can select the "Click here to select only this new music." link. From there, I can select the specific songs that I want uploaded. As shown in Figure 6–22, your selection starts at All Music, then to Artists (Kkat is the only one here), then to the work (*Fallout: Equestria*), and then to the list of individual songs, or audio chapters in this case. I check the boxes next to the songs that I wish to download, and my audio files are downloaded to the Kindle from my computer.

Figure 6–22. *Selecting music to upload to the Cloud Drive*

I find that this method of downloading is quite slow. It can take up to several hours before the song appears on my Kindle Fire device. For this reason, I highly recommend using a USB-to-micro-USB cord. The advantage is that the audio file will appear instantaneously, provided the transfer is done correctly. You can discover more about USB-to-micro-USB file transfers in Chapter 8.

It is easy to copy the audio file from your My Downloads folder and paste it into the Kindle Fire folder titled Music. You should see the new audio file appear in the Songs section right away.

All it really takes is going to the site with the download and downloading from there. You have to download it on the Kindle Fire if you want it to go from cloud to device.

Getting a Song from a CD onto Your Kindle Fire

There are many ways to get songs from a CD onto your Kindle Fire. The following steps are for using a PC with Window Media Player installed.

1. Insert the CD into the computer's CD drive.

2. Open Windows Media Player. You will see a list of songs on the CD, similar that shown in Figure 6–23.

3. Check the songs that you want from the CD, and then click Rip CD at the top of the menu.

Figure 6–23. *Selecting songs to rip from a music CD*

4. The selected tunes now appear in your Library. Eject the CD; you will not need it anymore.

5. Open your Cloud Player.

6. Select Upload Your Music.

7. You should see a window that looks similar to Figure 6–24. Click the "Click here to select only this new music." link.

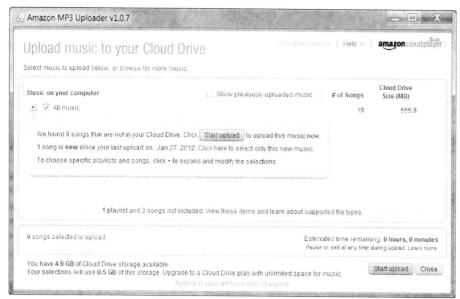

Figure 6–24. *Selecting music for your Cloud Drive*

8. Select by Artist the individual track or tracks that you want to add to the Cloud Player (see Figure 6–25).

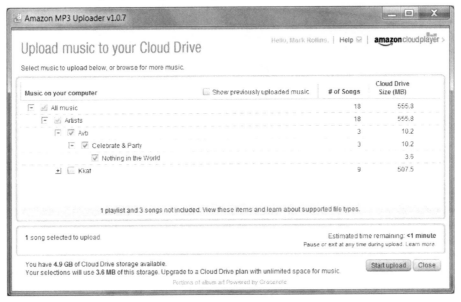

Figure 6–25. *I chose a song called "Nothing in the World" from the album* Celebrate & Party *by the group Avb.*

9. Select Start Upload. A bar shows that the song is uploading.

It may take several minutes before you are able to access the song on your device. From there, you can put it on your playlist.

Summary

The Kindle Fire makes it easy to get music from a computer to the device with an easy-to-use Cloud Player and MP3 Uploader that can be downloaded to your computer. The Uploader is able to search your computer for playlists and other audio files, and transfer them to the cloud.

Songs can be made to play in the background while you're doing other tasks on the Kindle Fire. You can also create and edit your playlists.

Finding and purchasing a song has never been easier thanks to the Music store's method of organization, which sorts music by Bestsellers, New Releases, and Genres. You can even sample a song before you buy it.

The Cloud Player is an online program that you can access while you are away from your Kindle Fire. It is simple to use and can sort your music in the way that is best for you.

Chapter 7

Video

Ever since streaming video came to the Internet, I watch fewer programs on television. I now wait for television episodes to appear on video content sites like Hulu. The future of video is clearly one where random channel surfing is a thing of the past and we only watch what we want to watch.

The Kindle Fire is well ahead of its time. In addition to being an electronic book and magazine reader and a music player, the Kindle Fire is a good way to see the latest and greatest in video. The video can be stored on the cloud. You can also go online and watch all your videos from an internet-connected computer; and if you have a compatible device on your home theater, you can watch your video content there as well.

Of course, you first have to buy or rent most of this video content. I say "most" because you can access a lot of video content free if you are an Amazon Prime member. Of course, an Amazon Prime subscription is about $79 per year. Other Kindle Fire video providers, including Netflix and Hulu Plus, also have subscription fees.

When you first access Video from the Home screen, you immediately go to the Video store (see Figure 7–1, left). If you click Library (see Figure 7–1, right), you experience nothing more than a nearly blank screen. I say that we should definitely start filling up that Library with some content at the store.

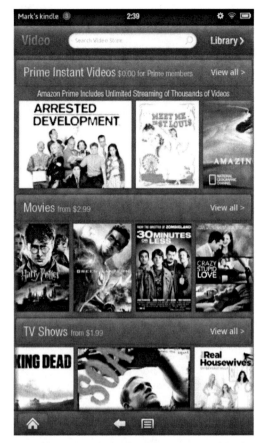

Figure 7–1. *The Kindle Video store and an empty Library*

The Kindle Video Store

When you go to the Video store, there are three horizontal "banners" that represent the types of video content that you can watch on your Kindle Fire or through your Amazon account. They are Prime Instant Videos, and Movies and TV Shows.

Amazon Prime Instant Videos

Thanks to the complimentary month of Amazon Prime benefits that came with the purchase of your Kindle, movies and TV shows are accessible for free streaming during this time. Tapping View All in the Prime Instant Videos section defaults to Movies (see Figure 7–2, left). Tap TV to see all the TV shows that are available (see Figure 7–2, right).

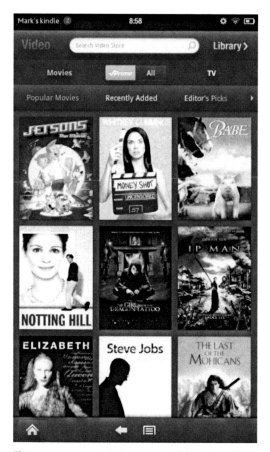

Figure 7–2. *Amazon's Prime Instant Video store for movies (left) and TV (right)*

Movies and TV include the following categories:

- *Popular Movies*: These are not necessarily the best movies/TV shows, or the latest, but they are "popular." They are the ones that users are watching the most.

- *Recently Added*: The newest films/TV shows.

- *Editor's Picks*: This is an interesting place to find films/TV shows. It includes categories that you have to see to believe.

- *All Genres*: This is where you can find all the genres for your shows, including the following:

  - Action & Adventure

  - Comedy

  - Documentary

  - Drama

- Foreign Films
- Sci-Fi & Fantasy

- *For the Kids*: The title really says it all; these movies are made for or can be enjoyed by a younger audience.

- *Holiday*: This genre might not always be available, but it includes Christmas movies.

- *TV Channels*: If you are looking for a certain television show and you know the network it's on, this is the place to look. Networks include the following:

  - ABC
  - Acorn Media
  - BBC
  - CBS
  - Fox
  - National Geographic
  - NBC
  - PBS
  - Sesame Workshop
  - Showtime

If you can't find what you were looking for on Prime through these category-narrowing searches, I suggest you use the search engine. I cannot guarantee that the video that you want is on Prime, but if it is, you are provided a screen with the option watch it (see Figure 7–3, left). Television shows provide the option to select a specific episode by season (see Figure 7–3, right). Tapping Purchase Options allows you to buy a movie or TV show.

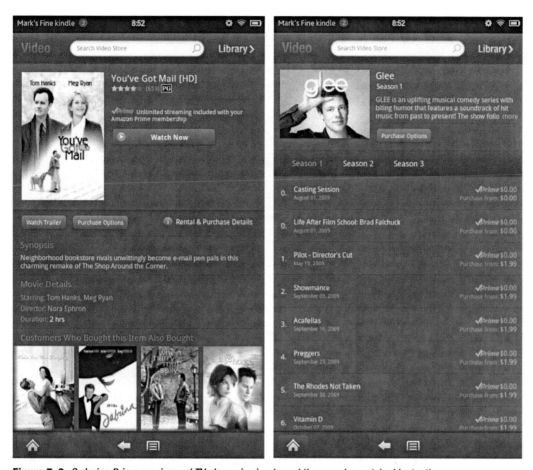

Figure 7–3. *Ordering Prime movies and TV shows is simple and they can be watched instantly.*

Movies and TV

Toggling from Prime to All provides a sample of Video offerings (see Figure 7–4).

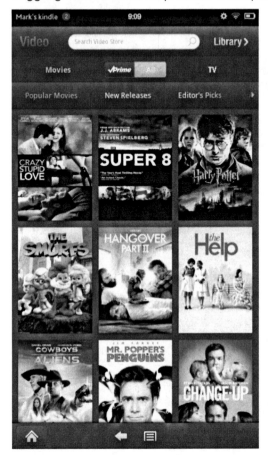

Figure 7–4. *Video available for Kindle Fire users—it's a lot*

The search engine is designed for finding virtually anything, assuming that the movie has been released to DVD and the TV show is similarly available.

There is also a category called Deals. Here, movie rentals are available for $1.99 or $2.99. Most newly-released movies cost $3.99 for a 48 hour rental. TV programs are available for $0.99 per episode; and TV seasons are available for $10 to $15. Most new television episodes are about $1.99; the price for entire seasons ranges from $34.99 to $49.99 for HD. Free TV extras are essentially free sneak previews.

Buying a Movie or TV Show

It is very easy to buy a movie or a TV show. Once you locate a video entry, tap the price next to 48 Hour Rental (see Figure 7–5). The transaction is automatically billed to your account. It is available for viewing on your Kindle, computer, or any other AV device compatible with Kindle Fire's viewer.

When you rent, you can store the video for a certain time period (usually a few weeks). However, the moment you begin to watch the video, the rental time begins. Conveniently, a video is automatically removed from your video list when the rental time expires, so you don't have to worry about late fees as with a traditional video rental store.

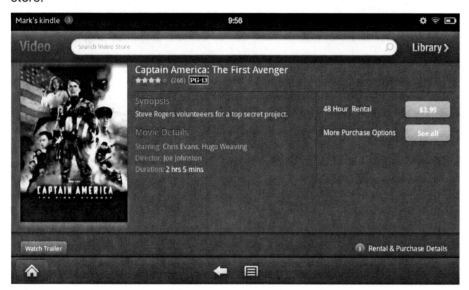

Figure 7–5. *A typical movie entry on the Kindle Fire (this one is not Prime)*

On the Kindle Fire, you have the option to buy or rent. Tap the See All button to the left of the More Purchase Options to reveal your choices (see Figure 7–6).

Figure 7–6. *Options for purchasing or renting a movie*

You can buy a TV show by episode or by entire season. For example, I know I want to buy a particular episode of *Community*, so I go to the search engine and type in the show's title (see Figure 7–7). I can select any one of the show's seasons, including its current one. The episode that I want is from Season 1, so I tap there.

Figure 7–7. *Searching for a specific video on the Kindle Fire Video store*

I can purchase *Community* Season 1 for $33.99 or $42.99 in HD (see in Figure 7–8, left). If I do, the entire season appears in my Library, and I can select which episode that I want to watch. Let's say that I am only interested in buying one episode. If I am not certain of the name of the episode that I want, I can scroll through the episode list and read the synopses. When I locate the one I want, I buy it; the typical price is $1.99.

The screen shows the name of the show and the title of the episode ("Modern Warfare" in Figure 7–8, right). The synopsis is always pretty brief, so to I tapped "more" to get a fuller description. The original air date, the runtime, and the network are also provided.

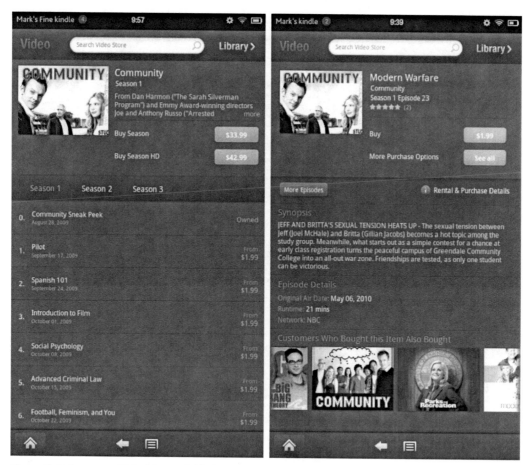

Figure 7–8. *A season of television available for purchase on the Kindle Fire*

As soon as I purchase the episode, I get the screen shown in Figure 7–9.

Figure 7–9. *Your options after buying a TV show*

When you purchase video, you have the option to Watch Now or Download. Downloading can only be done once. I will explain in the next section.

Watching a Video on the Kindle

Videos need to be watched in landscape mode. Touching the center of the screen opens up the option of play/pause. The bar next to it is for jumping to a particular scene. The volume control is at the top of the screen so that you don't have to go to the Quick Settings menu to adjust it.

One of the most helpful buttons is the Back Ten Seconds button in the upper-left corner. It is good for situations where you might have missed something; you get a quick rewind.

If you are concerned about whether you need to be online (synced with a valid Wi-Fi hot spot) to watch a video, it is certainly something to consider. Like the Newsstand, Books, and Music on the Kindle Fire, Videos has a Cloud or Device option (located at the top center of the screen).

The cloud is a massive storage space where you can keep an unlimited number of videos; but you have to be connected to the internet access it. This is a problem if you want to watch videos on long car trips or airplane flights and Wi-Fi is not available.

You must download videos onto your Kindle Fire in order to watch them when it is not connected to the internet. You can see in Figure 7–9 that the episode of *Community* that I purchased gave me that option. I simply tap the Download button, and, after a certain amount of time (depending on the video's length), the video is on my device, accessible without Wi-Fi.

If you want to check whether or not a certain video can be watched without Wi-Fi, simply tap Device on the Videos Library page; you should see it on the shelf. If it does not appear, try downloading again.

Your Online Video Account

One advantage to having a Kindle Fire is that you can watch videos that you own even if you don't have the device on hand. That's right. From a computer, you go to www.amazon.com/manageyourkindle, log in to your account, and click the Manage Your Videos section. You get a screen like the one shown in Figure 7–10.

Figure 7–10. *Watch your videos online from your computer*

There are several choices available, located on the tabs underneath the search engine. They include the following:

■ *Best Sellers*: Features some of the latest movies, the ones recently released on DVD and Blu-ray. If you are looking for recent movies, chances are this is the place to find them.

■ *Getting Started*: Shows you, according to Amazon.com, how to get started watching "over 100,000 movies and TV shows, including over 10,000 available with Amazon Prime, on a PC, Mac, [and] hundreds of compatible TVs".

■ *Watch on Your TV*: Tells you whether or not you can watch a video on another video-streaming device (like Roku). A link called "See out list of compatible devices" (see Figure 7–11) lists the devices compatible with your Kindle account. You may already have the capability of watching your Kindle video footage from your TV, Blu-ray player or other A/V device; all you may have to do is connect your device to a broadband connection.

Figure 7-11. *Watch on Your TV tab— discover if you have a compatible device*

■ *Prime Instant Videos*: Allows the Amazon Prime member access to videos instantly on his or her browser. Entire movies and seasons of television shows are available here, and if you are not certain whether it is available for viewing instantly, enter it in the search engine. A green button with a $0.00 price tag tells you that you can watch for free (see Figure 7-12). Click this button and the video opens in the browser. You also have the option of buying the episode or the entire season. Scroll down for a list of other episodes in the season, which you can download to watch when you are not connected to the internet.

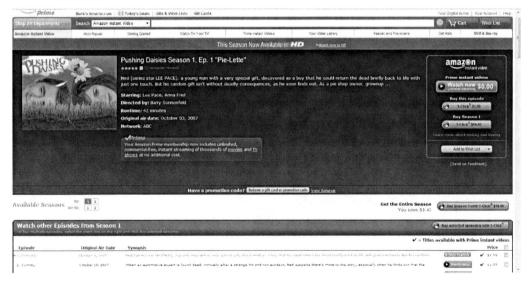

Figure 7-12. *Amazon Prime TV allows you to watch TV shows online*

- *Your Video Library*: What Managing Your Videos defaults to. In Figure 7–10, *Community* Season 1 is listed, but if I were to click it, I actually only have one episode. If I wanted to watch the episode on a browser instead of my Kindle Fire, it is as easy as clicking Watch Now. By the way, if I am watching an episode on one device, and then switch to the other, it resumes to where I left off. I can also buy more episodes from here.

- *Passes and Pre-orders*: If you have a special pre-order or TV pass, this is the place to use it. These can be purchased through Amazon.

- *Get Help*: Provides quick assistance if you are having trouble with Amazon Instant Video.

Other Methods of Watching Video

There is usually more than one way to do something on the Kindle Fire. Just as you can read a magazine via an app, or a book through some other method, you don't need to be in Video mode to watch a video.

YouTube and Other Video-Sharing Sites

One of the big problems with Apple products, such as the iPhone and the iPad, is that there is no Adobe Flash, which is a source of contention amongst Apple users. Although Apple does not seem to be warming up to Adobe Flash, it isn't a problem on the Kindle Fire! Apple requires a special app to run YouTube, but you can run YouTube directly from your browser (see Figure 7–13). Just go to the Web category and enter the YouTube URL, www.youtube.com. (More about the Web in Chapter 10.)

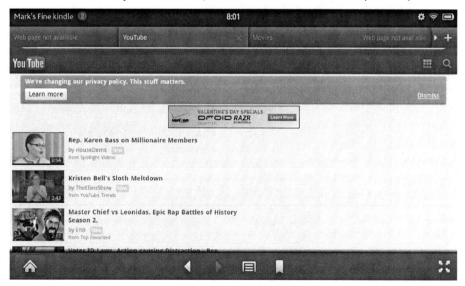

Figure 7–13. *YouTube on the Kindle Fire*

YouTube plays any video you care to see, and other video-sharing sites like Dailymotion (www.dailymotion.com) and Vimeo (www.vimeo.com) are also readily available for viewing. If you are having trouble playing videos, you might want to hit the Contents menu on the Kindle Fire's Web player. Tap Settings and scroll down to Enable Flash (see Chapter 10 for more information).

Crackle

Crackle (www.crackle.com) is one of my favorite places to watch movies and TV shows online (see Figure 7–14). Crackle works well on the Kindle Fire, but you might want to turn on your Flash Player if you are having problems viewing movies or TV shows. Be sure to check their selection of free videos before you buy or rent something elsewhere.

Figure 7–14. *Crackle, a good place to watch old movies and TV shows online on Kindle Fire's web browser*

Netflix

I found Netflix available on the App Store. The application is free to download, but you have to pay for everything you watch. Netflix offers one month free, so that is a bonus if you just want to try it out (see Chapter 9 for downloading new applications).

If you don't have a Netflix account, it is quite easy to get one. You can set one up on your computer or on the Kindle Fire Web. After the one-month free trial, it costs $7.99 a month to access their unlimited DVDs. To begin, fill out the Netflix subscription form (see Figure 7–15).

Figure 7–15. *The Netflix online subscription form*

When you open your account on the Kindle Fire, you see a prompt for an e-mail and password, as shown in Figure 7–16.

Figure 7–16. *The Netflix login screen on the Kindle Fire*

Once you log in, you should see a screen like the one shown in Figure 7–17.

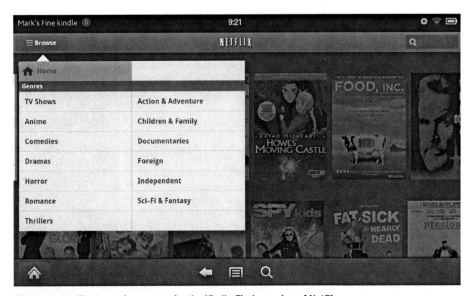

Figure 7-17. *The browsing screen for the Kindle Fire's version of Netflix*

The Netflix screen is very similar to the Amazon Kindle Video player. You can select movies by browsing the Genres menu, located in the upper-left corner, or using the search engine in the upper-right.

Touching a film poster reveals a button to add the movie to the Instant Queue (see Figure 7-18, left). Press play to view the movie.

Notice on my Home screen that there are videos that I am in the process of watching (see Figure 7-18, right). They are saved and waiting for me to press play to continue watching at exactly the point that I left off.

Netflix also provides recommendations. You can continuously scroll down to find more content.

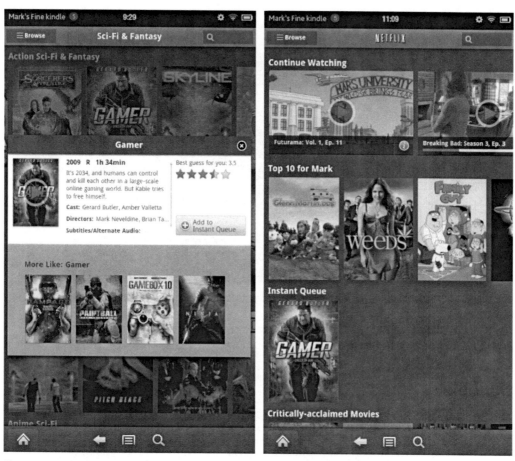

Figure 7-18. *Adding a movie to your Netflix queue (left), and then playing it (right)*

Playing a movie is very similar to playing one on Kindle Fire's Video, but Netflix offers the option for subtitles with a balloon icon in the bottom-right corner of the screen (see Figure 7–19).

Figure 7–19. *A Netflix movie on the Kindle Fire offers play/pause, tracking, and the option for subtitles.*

Netflix also allows you to play movies on your computer or any video gaming system, provided it is connected to the internet.

Hulu Plus

The popular Hulu Plus (www.hulu.com/plus) is also available on the Kindle Fire. It costs $7.99 a month. Like Netflix, you can try it out for free, but only for a week.

You need to set up an account on Hulu Plus before downloading (see Figure 7–20). Hulu requires you have a credit card or PayPal account along with a billing address and phone number.

Figure 7–20. *Starting a free trial on Hulu Plus*

You can also access Hulu Plus on your computer, and if you have an Android smartphone, you can download the app.

With Hulu Plus, you have the option of selecting from the following (see Figure 7–21, left):

■ *Free Gallery*: Allows you to watch certain videos without logging in.

■ *Log In*: Enter your e-mail and password to access programming.

■ *TV and Movies*: Prompts you to log in to access TV or movies.

When you log in, you get the following options (see Figure 7–21, right):

■ *TV and Movies*: Opens all the video content, including TV programs and full-length feature films.

■ *Queue*: Stores the videos that you select. Adding videos to the queue is simple (see Figure 7–22, left). Removing a video clip from the queue is as simple as pressing and holding.

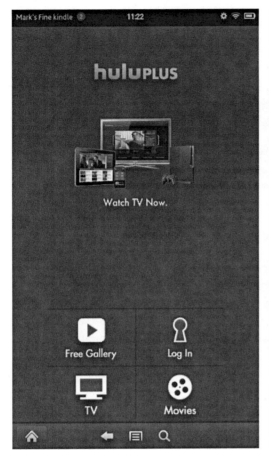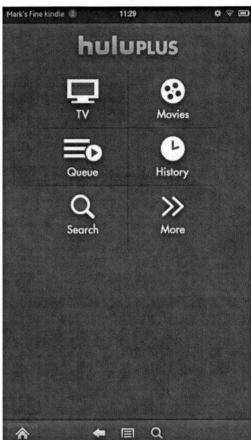

Figure 7–21. *Logging on to Hulu Plus on the Kindle Fire*

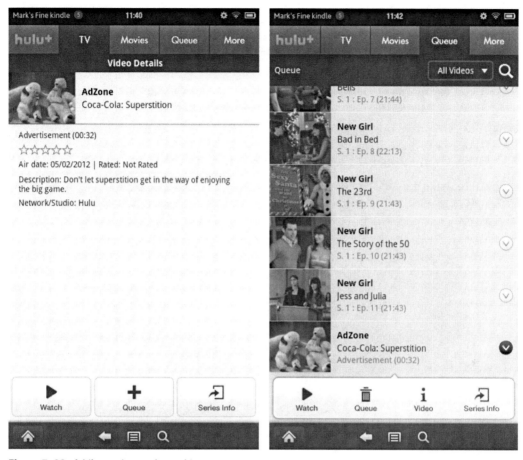

Figure 7–22. *Adding and removing a video on your queue*

- *History*: Lists all the shows that you have watched on Hulu, presented in order of viewing.

- *Search*: Provides searching capabilities for a particular show or movie.

- *More*: Provides additional settings, as well as some available elsewhere.

  - *Favorites*: Lists your Favorite TV shows.

  - *Account*: Provides information about your Hulu Plus account.

  - *Log Out*: Takes you completely out of the Hulu Plus application.

Summary

The Kindle Fire is definitely optimized for video. It is made so videos can be viewed and downloaded to it with ease. New Kindle Fire users have access to a free month of

Amazon Prime movies and TV shows. Otherwise, movies, as well as TV episodes or entire seasons, can be purchased or rented with instant transaction processing. These videos are also available offline, provided the user downloads to hisor her personal device.

Videos can be downloaded to the Kindle or viewed online through the user's Managing Your Videos account. This includes the videos on Amazon Prime.

When switching from the Kindle Fire to an internet-connected computer or another wired or wireless device, videos resume from where you left off. If you have the proper compatible video-streaming device, you can watch these videos on your television.

Kindle Fire users can also access video-sharing sites like YouTube and Crackle from the Web category. And, with a subscription, they can download apps for Netflix and Hulu Plus to watch video on their Kindle Fire, computer, or compatible AV device.

Chapter 8

Docs

We live in an age where we walk around with multiple devices like laptops, mobile phones, cameras, and MP3 players, with diverse content on each of them. Unless you can find some way to sync all your mobile devices together, you might get frustrated when you are trying to find a particular file. If you add a Kindle Fire to the mix, this easily adds to the confusion, but at least the Kindle Fire makes it easy to find a digital file like a video, audio, photo, or other type of document.

There is no USB-to-micro-USB cable that comes with the Kindle Fire. As I mentioned in Chapter 3, it is almost an unnecessary accessory for the Kindle Fire because it is possible to upload files to the Kindle Fire wirelessly. So no matter where you are, you can download files to your Kindle Fire, provided you have access to your files and a computer connected to the internet. Of course, you need to have your Kindle connected to a network to receive the file. Still, I recommend purchasing a USB-to-micro-USB cable simply because it makes downloading a file to and from the Kindle much faster.

Digital files like videos, photos, and music can be downloaded and then viewed in the Docs category on the Kindle Fire. The Docs category works best as a viewer of text-only documents. These files are viewed in Kindle format. Docs can actually hold any document you like, provided it is in the proper format.

I will explain how to organize your documents in the Docs category on the Home screen, and how to use your Kindle Fire as a place to store all kinds of files.

The Docs Shelf

Unlike Newsstand and Video, Docs has a default file that comes with your Kindle Fire— the *Kindle Fire User's Guide*. I recommend that you not delete the user's guide because it provides a lot of information about your Kindle Fire.

The rest of the Docs shelf is blank until you fill it with something. I filled my Docs shelf with things like my tax returns and other documents (see Figure 8–1, left). By the way, sometimes documents appear on your Docs shelf without any warning. For example, I once had a document warning me that my Amazon Prime subscription was ending.

You can also see on the top shelf in Figure 8–1 that *Catching Fire (The Second Book of the Hunger Games)* has expired. I checked out this book through my Amazon Prime membership; this is how the Kindle Fire lets you know that it expired. Don't be surprised if messages from Amazon show up in the Docs section, but don't expect a warning every time you do something with the Amazon Kindle Fire. The Docs section is not designed to be a messenger platform.

Figure 8–1. *The first document on the top shelf, the Kindle Fire User's Guide, comes with Docs on the Kindle Fire. Opening the document reveals the cover page (right).*

The Docs shelf features a By Recent button and a By Title button so that you can choose your method of organization.

Tapping the By Recent button sorts the files by order of use on the Kindle Fire, with the most recent document appearing last. For example, you can see that the *Kindle Fire User's Guide* is first on my Docs shelf (see Figure 8–2, left) because it was my first document.

Tapping By Title organizes your files alphabetically (see Figure 8–2, right).

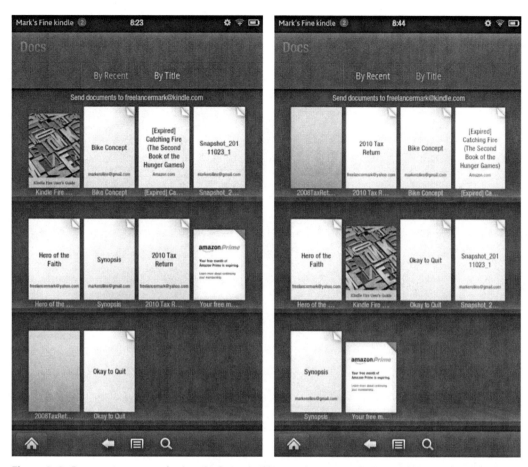

Figure 8–2. *Documents are organized on the Docs shelf in one of two ways: By Recent (left) and By Title (right)*

The buttons at the bottom of the screen include the Back button, which takes you back to the Home screen, or wherever you were previously.

The Contents button provides two options. The Docs category allows you to view in grid view (see Figure 8–3, left), the default, or list view (see Figure 8–3, right). Tap the Contents button to switch views.

Grid view works with thumbnails, and if the format of the document permits, there is a cover illustration. Otherwise, there is just a generic title, which is often the name of the file. The name also appears beneath the document.

There is an e-mail address on each of the documents. The e-mail address is where the document was sent from; documents are sent to your Kindle Fire via e-mail your Amazon account. I explain this later in the chapter.

At times, documents have a percentage number marked on them. This is because the Kindle Fire keeps track of how far along you are in reading a document.

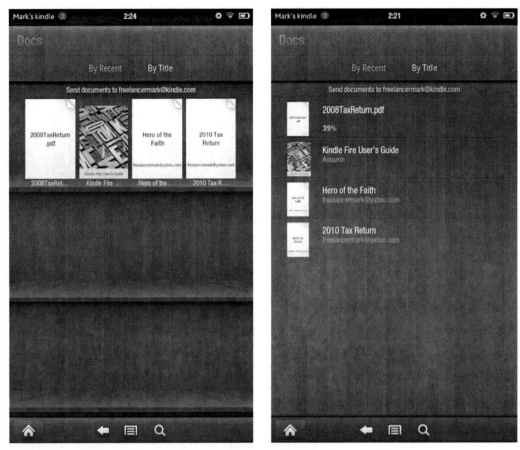

Figure 8–3. *The Docs shelf shown in grid view (left) and list view (right)*

The Docs search engine is meant for searching the titles of documents, not the content. So if you have a file in Docs about trucks, for example, don't perform a search on "trucks" and expect to find the document unless the word "trucks" is in the title.

Pressing and holding a document on the shelf opens a window that allows you to Add to Favorites or Delete (see Figure 8–4). It is similar to press-and-hold functions in the Newsstand and Books categories. I noticed that the *Kindle Fire User's Guide* cannot be removed in this fashion.

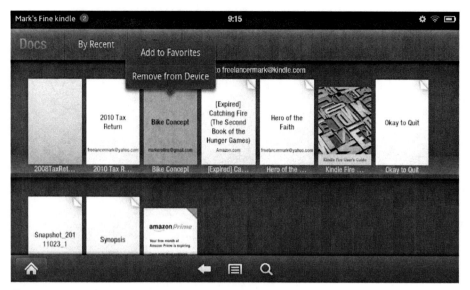

Figure 8–4. *Pressing and holding a file on the Docs shelf*

Reading a Document in Docs

Reading a document on the shelf is quite similar to reading an e-book, provided that it is in a certain format. Adobe Portable Document Format (PDF) files, for example, transfer seamlessly because PDF documents have fixed pages. This is different from an e-book, where a particular page location is different than it is in the print version. This is due to differences in the font sizes.

Unfortunately, PDF documents don't have the options that are typically available on the Contents button. With e-books, the Contents button allows you access specific pages, such as the cover or first page, or a particular page, or to furthest page read.

A typical document page in Docs looks like the one shown in Figure 8–5.

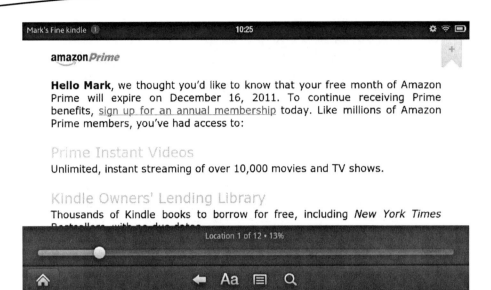

Figure 8–5. *A typical document page*

Certain formats also support the Text button (Aa), which changes the Font Style and Typeface. The text highlighting feature, discussed in the Newsstand and Books chapters, is also supported. It allows you to make notes on sections, highlight, and search Wikipedia and Google.

Bookmarks (in certain formats) work by pressing on the upper-right corner (see Figure 8–5), as done with e-books. Bookmarks, as well as the notes and highlights, can be found in the Contents menu.

Wirelessly Transferring to the Kindle Fire

Since the Kindle Fire does not come with a USB-to-micro-USB connector out of the box, you have the option of transferring digital files wirelessly. Fortunately, this can be accomplished quite easily.

Your Kindle Fire E-mail Address

As a new Kindle user, you have a Send-to-Kindle e-mail address that is good for sending documents to your Kindle Fire. It always ends with @kindle.com. I don't remember setting up one, but it took the first part of my primary e-mail address and created one automatically. This address is apparently made with the device registration.

If you don't know your Kindle Fire e-mail address, tap the Quick Settings icon and then tap My Account (see Figure 8–6).

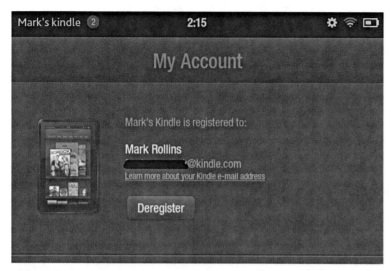

Figure 8–6. *Your Send-to-Kindle e-mail address is found at My Account*

If you want to edit your personal address in Kindle, go to the Manage Your Kindle page at www.amazon.com/manageyourkindle. After clicking Personal Documents from the navigation bar on the left, you'll come to a screen similar to the one in Figure 8–7.

Figure 8–7. *An online account for managing your Kindle*

I will get into more detail on what you can do on this screen later, but for now, let's get back to changing information on your account. On the left navigation bar, click Personal Document Settings (see Figure 8–8).

Figure 8–8. *Managing your personal account settings online*

You can manage your personal account settings from one place, with three options for editing.

- ▨ *Send-to-Kindle E-mail Settings*: Enables you to change the first part of your e-mail address.

- ▨ *Personal Document Archiving*: Enables personal documents sent to your Kindle to also be added to your Kindle library.

- ▨ *Approved Personal Document E-mail List*: Allows you to approve the e-mail addresses that you want to send documents to. You can enter whatever e-mail addresses that you like here.

You can send documents from your Kindle e-mail account, just like a Google, Yahoo, or any other account. All that is required is to attach the document to the e-mail.

Figure 8–9 shows an e-mail being sent to a Kindle account through Gmail.

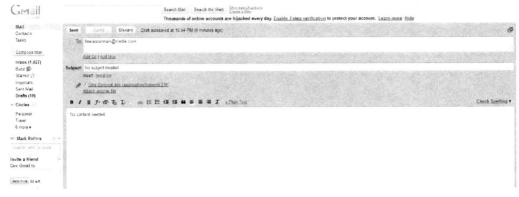

Figure 8–9. *E-mailing a document to a Kindle account*

When e-mailing to a Kindle account, no subject or message is needed; just an attachment and the proper e-mail address to the Kindle.

Keep in mind that only certain file formats are supported, as follows:

- For documents, use AZW, AXW1, TXT, MOBI (unprotected), PRC, and DOC formats.

- For audio supported within music, use AAC LC/LTP, HE-AACv1 (AAC+), HE-AACv2 (enhanced AAC+), AMR-NB (.3gp), AMR-WB (.3gp), MP3, MIDI, OggVorbis (or .ogg), and PCM/WAVE (.wav).

- For images, use JPEG, PNG, GIF, and BMP.

- For video, use H.263 (.3gp, mp4), H264 AVC (.3gp, .mp4), MPEG 4SP/ASP (.3gp), and VP8 (.webm).

The following are other restrictions for e-mailing a document:

- The file size should be 50 MB or less.

- The e-mail should contain no more than 25 attached personal documents.

- E-mail must target fewer than 15 distinct Send-to-Kindle e-mail addresses.

- Should the Kindle Fire not be connected wirelessly, e-mail is stored for 60 days. An attempt to deliver to the device is made when wireless connectivity is restored.

- If you are sending a PDF file, Amazon recommends that you write "convert" in the subject line; the file will be converted into Kindle format.

According to Amazon, it takes about five minutes to send a 5 MB document in a supported file format to arrive on a Kindle Fire. I found that it took a lot longer than that. At this writing, there have been complaints about internet problems with the Kindle Fire, but I am not certain whether this is the cause.

Once you send the document, it first goes to Pending Deliveries, which you can access on the left navigation bar of the Manage Your Kindle page. The number of files awaiting deliveries is shown, as seen in Figure 8–10. You can also view the successful deliveries.

Figure 8–10. *Once a document is sent, it is briefly available for viewing in Pending Deliveries*

It actually took hours before documents that I sent via e-mail showed up on the Docs shelf. I will discuss a quicker method using the USB-to-micro-USB connection soon, but for now, I want to finish my discussion on Personal Documents.

Managing Your Personal Account Online

As shown in Figure 8–7, most of your documents are listed in the Personal Documents section. Documents sent by Amazon, like the *Kindle Fire User's Guide*, and documents that work by wired transfers, as I will explain later, do not appear here.

There is a plus sign beside each document. Tapping it shows the file size, title, author (origin of e-mail), date (when it arrived on the Kindle Fire), and an Actions button. Tapping Actions offers two options: Deliver to My… and Delete from Library (see Figure 8–11).

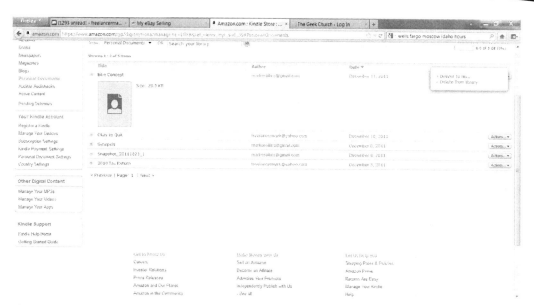

Figure 8–11. *The first row's Actions button reveals more information on the online Personal Documents page*

I found that Delete from Library actually took a while to delete a file from my Kindle; but, like transferring a file to the Kindle Fire, be patient and just consider the action done.

The Deliver to My… option sends the file to any other Kindle that you have connected to your computer.

Transferring Documents to the Kindle by Cable

As I mentioned in Chapter 3, you need a lot of accessories for your Kindle Fire. If you want to move your content around in a wired fashion, purchase a USB-to-micro-USB connector. As much as I would have liked the Kindle Fire to come with one, it is unfortunately sold separately, but readily available on Amazon itself. You may not even need to buy one; if you have other mobile devices, you may already have a compatible USB-to-micro-USB cable. For example, my Droid X charger, minus its connectable USB plug, works just fine.

After connecting the USB/micro-USB cord to your computer, you should see a graphic like the one shown in Figure 8–12 on your Kindle Fire screen.

Figure 8–12. *The Kindle Fire screen when connected to a computer*

You should see a window similar to Figure 8–10 on your computer. I found that it took a while for my Windows 7 laptop to recognize the Kindle Fire. Depending on your operating system, you might see a window like the one shown in Figure 8–13.

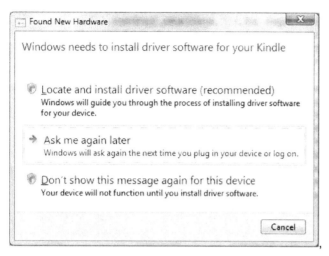

Figure 8-13. *You may need to install driver software the first time you connect your Kindle Fire to your computer via USB-to-micro-USB cable.*

Eventually, my computer figured out that a Kindle Fire was plugged into it. When you connect to your computer, you will likely experience a window similar to the one shown in Figure 8-14. (It may not look exactly like this; it depends on your operating system and the programs that you have installed.)

Figure 8–14. *Your computer recognizing the Kindle Fire after you plug it in via USB-to-micro-USB connector*

The Mixed Content Options window offers many ways to get programs from your Kindle Fire to your computer. For example, I discovered that hitting the Play button caused anything compatible with Windows Media Player to begin playing. This includes music, video, pictures, recorded TV, and other media. I could advance or rewind it if I wanted, but I quickly discovered that I didn't know how my computer even ordered it. If you open your Windows Media Player, locate your Kindle on the column to the left (see Figure 8–15). Open it to start playing media files the way you want to hear them.

Figure 8–15. *Opening the media files on Windows Media Player (Windows 7)*

The Mixed Content Options window provides other ways to get files quickly from the Kindle Fire to your computer. For example, when I used the Import Pictures and Videos Using Windows option, I found a window in the corner of my computer, like the one shown in Figure 8–16.

Figure 8–16. *Importing pictures and videos using Videos after plugging in your Kindle Fire*

While I admire the automatic process that some of these options give for downloading pictures and other media files to my computer, I only want certain files transferred to and from my Kindle. Note in Figure 8–14 that the General Options area offers the choice to simply Open Folder to View Files Using Windows Explorer.

Once you have opened the files, your window should look similar to Figure 8–17, showing all the folders.

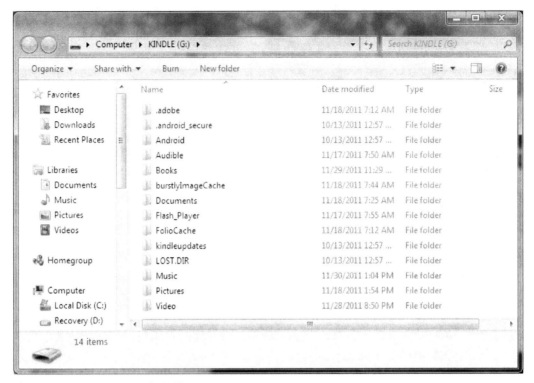

Figure 8–17. *Folders on the Kindle Fire*

From here, it is pretty easy to drag and drop files to the proper place. Any text-based document files, such as a Word file or a type listed earlier in the chapter, goes into Documents. Music is transferred to the Music folder, image files go into the Photos folder, and video into the Video folder.

I'm not certain I can suggest editing your documents this way, but if you know where your files are located, this might be the way to go.

I highly recommend moving pictures with wired transfers rather then sending them via e-mail.

Summary

Not only is the Kindle Fire a place to view magazines, newspapers, books, and videos, but it also allows you to read many types of documents. The user can transfer a document to his Kindle via e-mail attachment. Amazon gives Kindle users a special e-mail account for this purpose. Only certain files can be read on the Kindle, however, and there are other restrictions to sending files as well. After you e-mail a file to your Kindle, it may take a while before it appears.

The Kindle Fire can use a USB-to-micro-USB cable to transfer computer files in a drag-and-drop method. I recommend putting files into the folders designated for them, such as videos in Videos, photos in Photos, and so on.

All the documents on the Kindle are stored on the Docs shelf, and are for viewing only. Occasionally, Amazon puts documents on the shelf, including warnings about subscriptions about to come to an end. These particular files cannot be managed by the user, but anything sent wirelessly to the Kindle can be managed online.

Chapter 9

Apps

It seems like we have always lived in an age where "there's an app for that," but it really is a pretty recent development. The app market has been booming over the past five years, and iOS along with Android have led the charge.

Having the Kindle Fire capable of apps, especially Android apps, creates a device that can do potentially anything. The end result is a lot of choice in the programs that users want to suit their lifestyles.

When I first heard that the Amazon Appstore for Android wasn't going to be the same as the Android Market for smartphones and other tablets, I have to admit that I, along with many others, was quite disappointed. You see, Android's success has come from it being open source, and apps put on the Android Market do not need permission, unlike iOS. The Amazon Appstore for Android does require a sign-off from Amazon in order to make it to their marketplace, however, the Amazon app market is quite diverse, and more apps are being introduced to it every day. By the way, one of the reasons why Amazon personally checks out each application is to test for malware and other things that would create a negative user experience.

The Kindle Fire comes with all kinds of apps; some are shown in Figure 9–1. Like the Favorites shelf, the Apps shelf is seemingly infinite. Kindle Fire's Apps also offers the Cloud or Device option, but most of your apps will be on your device. The only ones that should be in the cloud are apps that you have bought, but have not installed. There are a few of these apps on the Kindle Fire's default apps (with an arrow on the icon). I will explain how to download them later.

You can also sort apps with the By Recent button, which places your most recently used apps first (see Figure 9–1, left). By Recent is a good way to organize your apps if you are in the habit of returning to the same ones. I know that there are several apps that I can't live without, and it is handy knowing that they are always in the same location on the shelf.

You can also sort your apps alphabetically using the By Title option (see Figure 9–1, right).

Figure 9–1. *Sorting apps By Recent (left) and By Title (right)*

Eventually, you will have several apps on the shelf and will have to scroll down to find them. At the bottom of the screen are a few buttons, including Home, Back, and Search. Home and Back have the same function as in other categories. The search engine is designed to search your Apps shelf, not the apps store. Entering keywords narrows you down the shelf to the app that you want. You can see how it works in Figure 9–2. Entering "an" gives you access to apps that start with those two letters or have those two letters in the title.

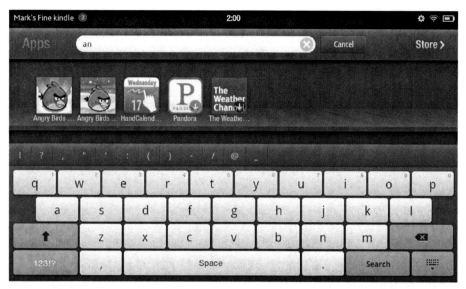

Figure 9–2. *The search engine for the Apps Library shelf is good for finding an app that you already have*

There is nothing here that you haven't seen in other categories, but you want to check out the Android Market by tapping Store in the upper-right corner (see Figure 9–2). This brings you to the Amazon Appstore for your Kindle Fire (see Figure 9–3).

Figure 9–3. *The Amazon Appstore for Android for the Kindle Fire—you should really get to know it*

Finding an App on the Amazon Appstore for Android

The Amazon Appstore for Android features a Free App for the Day. This is worth checking out every day, just so you can see what application is available at no cost. I found some really good games this way, including EA's version of *Monopoly*. Unfortunately, the Free App of the Day is always a mystery, so it's like Forrest Gump's box of chocolates: you never know what you are going to get.

There are also listings by Top Paid, Top Free, and Top Rated there (see Figure 9–3).

Finger swiping to the right allows you to see all the apps categories. These categories include the following:

- *Top*: Appears as soon as you open the Amazon Appstore for Android. You see some examples in Figure 9–3, including the very popular game *Where's My Water*. The Top apps change on a regular basis.

- *New*: Lists some of the latest apps. There are no Top Paid and Top Free lists. Like the Top Apps, this list changes regularly.

- *Games*: Everything that you want to play. Includes some specific genres to help you find the type of game that you are looking for, including the famous *Angry Birds* and *Where's My Water.*

  - *Action*: Any game with fighting and/or quick reflexes. Examples include *Fruit Ninja* (a game where you cut fruit with a finger swipe) and *Ninjump* (where you play a Ninja who travels up between two walls).

  - *Adventure*: Relates RPG (role-playing games) and types that place you in a different scenario. Examples include *The Mystery of the Crystal Portal* (a game where you find objects in a messy room) and *Galactic Striker* (a game where you are flying a spaceship blasting asteroids by steering the Kindle Fire with the built-in accelerometer).

  - *Arcade*: Games played in a 1980s-style standup arcade. Includes all versions of *Angry Birds* and classics like *Pac-Man*.

  - *Board*: Apps based on tabletop board games. Examples include tic-tac-toe, chess, checkers, backgammon, and family favorites like *Monopoly*, *Scrabble*, and *The Game of Life* (Kindle Edition).

  - *Cards*: Apps played with a normal 52-card deck, such as solitaire and freecell, as well other famous card games like *UNO*.

  - *Casino*: If you play it in Vegas, then you can find it here. Includes various versions of blackjack and slot machine apps.

- *Casual*: As far as I can tell, these are gaming apps to pass the time away. Includes games like *Paper Toss*, where you fling a virtual piece of paper into a garbage can, and *Jewels*, which is essentially a free version of *Bejeweled*, the immensely popular mobile game.

- *Educational*: I suppose this could be defined as any game that helps you learn or anything that requires thinking and not reflex action to win. Includes games like *Memory Trainer* or *What's Different*.

- *Kids*: Designed for children. Examples include *Kids Match'em and Pet Them: Baby Animals Edition*. Don't be surprised if you find an addictive game that you, the adult, love to play.

- *Multiplayer*: Games that require two or more players. Includes *Online Racer* and *Glow Hockey 2 Pro*, which is a lot like playing air hockey on a Kindle Fire touchscreen.

- *Music*: Thanks to the popularity of video games like *Guitar Hero* and *Rock Band*, there are many games that require the user to keep the beat of music. The mobile versions of the popular franchises and non-franchise music games like *mPiano*.

- *Puzzles and Trivia*: Think of crossword puzzles, Sudoku, and games of that nature; not to mention popular games like *Where's My Water* and *Cut the Rope*.

- *Racing*: Where would gaming be without racing games? Any game where you are in a car, motorcycle, or similar competing against other players, real or virtual. Titles here would include *Drag Racing* and *Dead Rider Lite*.

- *Role Playing*: Games where you play a character in a completely different world. Includes *Dungeon Defenders: Second Wave* and interesting multiple-choice games like *Choice of the Dragon* or *Choice of Romance*.

- *Sports*: Games based on sports or any activity that involves physicality. There are often interesting variations like *Cubicle Golf* or *Hockey Fight Lite*.

- *Strategy*: Games where players must not only think about their next move, but think several moves ahead to beat other players or a computer. These include many "towers of defense" games, and games using troops, weapons, and other war machines to stop opposing armies.

- *Recommended for You*: Amazon figures out games you might like to recommend games that you might want to play.

- *Entertainment*: Ranges from Netflix and Hulu Plus to drawing pads and anything designed to entertain. Yes, it is an extremely broad topic. Examples include *Stadium Horn Free*, TV.com, and *Little Piano*. Entertainment is different from Games because the element of competition is removed. Like Games, it ranks the Top and Recommended for You.

- *Lifestyle*: Difficult to precisely define; apps made to make our lives easier. Includes the following:

  - *Home & Garden*: Apps used in the home or in the backyard. Cooking and other kitchen-related apps are fair game here, as well as other home activities like gardening, woodworking, or sewing. Examples include *Green Lawns Made Easy*, *Paint Colors*, and *Cross Stitch Fabric Calculator*.

  - Self-Improvement: Apps for inspiration and gaining wisdom. Examples include Wise Proverbs Daily, Motivational Quotes, and Qi Gong Meditation Relaxation.

  - *Astrology*: Daily horoscopes. Includes *My Horoscope*, tarot, and various fortune-telling apps.

  - Relationships: Relates to romance, sex, or love. Includes Love Calculator, 101 Romantic Ideas, and Marriage Builders Radio.

  - *Hair & Beauty*: Apps designed to improve one's life cosmetically. Examples include *Makeup* and *SkinApp*.

  - *Celebrity*: Gossip and looking into the lives of celebrities. Includes *Gossiper* and *SpiritualLite*.

  - *Quizzes & Games*: Differs from regular trivia or anything found in Games. These are generally questions and answers to learn something more. Examples include *Random Life Facts* and *Show of Hands*, an anonymous polling app.

  - *Advice*: Apps to help guide. Examples range from daily Bible devotions to random guidance. Examples include *Beautiful Life Quotes* and *Dream Journal Pro*.

  - *Parenting*: Relates to raising children. Examples include *Popular Baby Names* and *My Baby Phone*.

- *News and Weather*: Considering that most people use their Kindle Fire to read newspapers, it makes sense to have apps for this category. It includes the following:

  - *World*: World news. Examples include Yahoo! for Android and PressReader.

▨ *US*: Focuses on news in the United States. National news apps include *USA Today 24/7 Free App Edition*. Lottery results apps like Mega Millions and Powerball are also included here.

▨ *Newspapers*: Oddly enough, my Kindle Fire gives me a message saying that "there are no apps in this category that are compatible with your device." You might want to check the Newsstand if you want to look in on this option.

▨ *Business*: Business news, including AP Mobile, *The Street*, and Yahoo! News.

▨ *Politics*: Political news. Examples include *The Huffington Post* and *Meet the Press*.

▨ *Entertainment*: Popular entertainment journals include *Urban Gossip Free* and *Hip Hop News*.

▨ *Sports*: As with Newspapers, there doesn't seem to be apps associated with this category. Perhaps this is coming soon?

▨ *Science & Tech*: Apps related to technological and scientific fields. Examples include *CNET News* and *Tech Crunch Reader*.

▨ *Health*: Examples include *Filtr Health*, which gives personalized health news alerts via mobile device.

▨ *Weather*: What good is a mobile device if it doesn't give the weather forecast? Examples include AccuWeather and The Weather Channel for Android.

▨ *Utilities*: Apps to help you out. These include the following:

▨ *Battery Savers*: Most Android smartphone users download a program known as *Advanced Task Killer*. Programs like these ensure that the device battery isn't using up too much power. Other examples include *Gemini App Manager*, *PowerWiFi*, and *Badass Battery Monitor* (ranked number one at this writing).

▨ *Alarms and Clocks*: Since the Kindle doesn't have an alarm clock accessible from its Home screen, you should download an app for one. Examples include *Touch Timer* and *Alarm Clock Xtreme*.

▨ *Calculators*: Why not use the Kindle Fire as a calculator? Examples include *Scientific Graphing Calculator* and *Karl's Mortgage Calculator*.

▨ *Calendars*: The Kindle Fire doesn't include a default calendar app, so you might want to download an app to help keep track of dates and times. Examples include *Cozi Family Organizer*, *NoteCalendar*, and *Countdown*.

- *Notes*: Use your Kindle Fire for taking notes (other than the note-taking tools in Books and Docs). Includes Notepad and Evernote.

- *Social Networking*: Apps include Twitter, LinkedIn, and Tumblr.

All Categories

Everything is here, including the following:

- *Books & Readers*: There's more than one way to read a book or graphic novel on a Kindle Fire! Examples include *Logos Bible Software*, *Goodreads*, and *Harold and the Purple Crayon Lite*.

    - *Comic Strips*: I could not find any actual comic strips like in the traditional newspaper Sunday funnies, but I did find apps like *Best Riddles* and *British Slang*.

    - *Manga*: Manga is a style of comics and animation that originated in Japan. Examples include *SManga*.

- *City Info*: Travel apps for certain cities. Examples include *Urbanspoon* and *World Explorer*. Cities covered include the following:

    - New York

    - Chicago

    - San Francisco

    - Boston

    - Dallas

    - Seattle

    - Phoenix

    - Philadelphia

    - Los Angeles

    - Miami

- *Communication*: Most of these apps are for e-mail and IM messaging. Examples Yahoo! Mail and the Trillian IM organizer.

- *Cooking*: Apps to use in the kitchen, including *Good Recipes*, *Allrecipes.com Dinner Spinner for Android*, and *Chef's Kitchen Timer*. I suggest using some sort of stand and screen cover if you are using while cooking.

- *Education*: Apps for learning all sorts of subjects, including the following:

- *Language*: Language-learning apps. Examples include *Spanish in a Month* and *Free French 24/7*. Also includes apps for learning basic English, like *Baby Learning ABC*.

- Math: Includes apps like Kid Math Game, Graphic Calculator, and Multiplication Rap 2x.

- Reading: Examples include Toddler ABC Flashcards, Word-A-Licious Lite, and Sight Words for Reading.

- Science: Examples include Moon Phase Pro, Periodic Table, and Biology FlashCards.

- *Test Guides*: While you might not be able to find any SAT prep apps here, you can find things like *Synonyms-Vocabulary*, *Flash Cards*, and *AB Vocabulary Builder*.

- *Writing*: I wasn't able to find anything to help me write this book, but I was able to find some things to help with vocabulary and spelling, including *Painless Spelling Challenge*, *Writing Rules*, and *123Slate*.

- *History*: I really didn't find many apps related to traditional school history, but there are very interesting studying apps like *gFlash+* and *StudyBlue Flashcards*. Traditional history apps include *U.S. Presidents*.

- *Entertainment*: Examples include Netflix, Hulu Plus, and Little Piano.

- *Finance*: Apps on fiscal matters. Sub-categories include the following:

  - *Accounting*: Help with personal taxes or budgeting. Examples include *TurboTax SnapTax*, *Quickbooks Mobile*, and *Budget Helper*.

  - *Banking*: I found a lot of apps related to specific banks like Chase Mobile and Discover Mobile, plus other interesting apps like TAN Manager and EMI Calculator.

  - *Finance*: Apps that are budgetary in nature, including Virtual Calculator, *iQuick DebtPayoff*, and *Finance and CFA Toolkit*.

  - *Investing*: Interested in Wall Street and the stock market? Then you want to check out these apps, which include *Bloomberg*, *Stock Alert*, and *Commodities*.

  - *Money & Currency*: Apps for the world traveler or those just on the road. Here you find *Tip Cow Free* (for calculating tips), *Bill Reminder*, and *Currency Converter*.

  - *Personal Finance*: A "miscellaneous" sub-category for finance. Examples include personal financing apps simply called Money, EasyMoney, and Checkbook.

- *Health & Fitness*: Apps to help with dieting and ways of keeping physically fit. They include the following:

  - *Diet & Weight Loss*: Designed for those wanting to count every calorie. Examples include *Calorie Counter* and *Diet Tracker* by MyFitnessPal and *Fast Food Nutrition Lite*.

  - *Exercise & Fitness*: For those into the "no pain, no gain" approach to dieting and long for a good workout. Apps include *Yoga Guru*.

  - *Medical*: First aid and personal health. Examples include *Baby Care, Prognosis: Your Diagnosis* and *Med Facts*.

  - *Sleep Trackers*: A lot of medical problems are a result of problems with sleep. Apps include *Sound Sleep (Music Therapy), Restful Sleep Deluxe Edition*, and *mySleepAnalyzer*.

  - *Pregnancy*: As a parent of three children, I understand (not fully) that having a baby can change everything, so you might like an app to help out with expecting your new arrival. This includes *BabyCenter, My Pregnancy Today, Baby Steps*, and *Labor and Contraction Timer*.

  - *Meditation*: Health and fitness apps to help the mind and body. Examples include *Inspiring Quotes, Insight Timer-Meditation Timer*, and *ConZentrate Free*.

- *Kids*: Lots of apps to keep the non-adults entertained and/or educated. The sub-categories include the following:

  - Reading: Apps to help children read; some are books. They include iStoryBooks, My First Words Lite, and Sports Illustrated Kids Magazine.

  - *Writing*: Apps to help kids learn to write, as well as slate apps to help tiny hands draw. Examples include *Letters and Numbers, Magic Slate HD*, and the *My First Words* series for many languages.

  - Alphabet: Apps for learning the alphabet. These apps include Connect the Dots & Color, ABC Interactive Lite, and ABC for Kids.

  - *Math*: Focuses on teaching numbers to growing little minds with apps like *My First Puzzles: Snakes Lite, A+ Times Table*, and *Math Training for Kids*.

  - *Science*: Parents who want to create genuine little Einsteins should check out these apps, which include *Science Fun to Go* and *Pet My Dinosaur*.

- History: App examples include Dino Digger and American History Books Free.

- *Language*: Apps designed to help a child's spelling, speaking, and writing skills. Examples include *Baby Sign and Learn Free* and *Droid Spell*.

- *Animals*: Animal-themed apps that are fun and educational. They include *BingAnimal* and *Techitect Pets*.

- *Popular Characters*: Apps connected to characters that kids love, from *The Cat in the Hat* to Santa Claus.

- *Magazines*: Apps for your popular magazines, including *People*, *Glamour*, and *Time*.

- *Music*: Differs from the Music category for playing music on your Kindle Fire. It includes the following sub-categories:

  - *Artists*: I didn't find a lot of specific musical artists here, but a variety of apps like *Free Time* and *VEVO*.

  - *Instruments*: For those who want to use their Kindle Fire like an electronic instrument. Examples include *Perfect Piano*, *Pitch Perfect*, and *Drum Pad Pro*.

  - *Radio*: Internet radio is a popular way of listening to music. Examples include *Pandora* and *Slacker Radio*.

  - *Songbooks*: Apps for those looking to play or sing music. Examples include *Lyric Pad* and *Music Note*.

  - *Music Player*: A way to play music beyond the Kindle Fire music player. These apps include *Rhapsody*, *Winamp*, and complex ones like the *FREEdi YouTube Player*.

- *Navigation*: Even though there is no GPS functionality on the Kindle Fire, that doesn't mean you can't get some limited navigation with apps like *MapQuest* and *Compass*.

- *Novelty*: Apps that are fun and interesting. Examples include *Spirograph*, *Magic 8 Ball*, and *Panic Button*.

- *Photography*: Apps to improve photographs with touch-ups and other artistic methods. Examples includes *Picasso*, *TouchUp Lite- Photo Editor*, and *PicsArt Photo Studio*.

- *Podcasts*: Podcasting apps like *MyPOD Podcast Manager Free*, *ACast*, and *TWiT Play*.

- *Productivity*: Apps designed to help you get things done. They include *Adobe Reader*, *KeepTrack Pro*, and *ColorNote Notepad Notes*.

- *Real Estate*: Apps on property values and other real estate topics. Examples include the popular *Zillow* and *Trulia Real Estate*.

- *Reference*: As a writer, I keep a few books within reach so I can look up certain facts needed for my work. Considering that the Kindle Fire has apps like dictionary, *World Map FREE*, and even the Bible, perhaps I can use these books in digital form.

- *Ringtones*: I'm not certain why this is a category; it isn't like the Kindle Fire has a phone. You might be able to use these sounds for other things. The subcategories include the following:

    - Pop
    - Rap
    - R&B
    - Rock
    - Country
    - Latin
    - Dance & Electronic
    - Christian
    - Soundtracks
    - Collegiate
    - TV
    - Voicetones
    - Comedy
    - Classical
    - Sound Effects
    - Sports
    - Jazz & Standards

- *Shopping*: For those who like shopping online and want to take their experience to the Kindle Fire. Examples include the *Official eBay Android App*, the *Coupons App*, and *Etsy for Android*.

- *Sports*: Apps related to sports and sports statistics, including the following:

    - Football
    - Baseball
    - Basketball

- Hockey

- NCAA

- Golf

- UFC

- Boxing

- Soccer

- Tennis

- *Themes*: I really couldn't find many apps here; it doesn't appear that the Kindle Fire is big on "themes" like Windows.

  - *Travel*: Those intending to take their Kindle Fire on the road can use these for traveling, provided they have access to Wi-Fi.

  - *Flight*: A good way to make flight plans. There are also apps for doing things on the plane. Examples include *FlightView Free*, FitPlan.com mobile, and *Cope with Jet Lag*.

  - *Hotels*: While you are booking a flight, you should take time to book a hotel with *HotelTonight, Hotels for Tablets*, and more.

  - *Auto Rental*: Ironically, these aren't really the best of auto rentals, as I could only find one related to car rentals. They have other apps worth checking out.

  - *Trip Planner*: For your travel itinerary, check here for apps like *TripAdvisor* and *TripIt Travel Organizer*.

  - *Currency Guides*: There are no apps found here, but you might want to look under Finance: Money and Currency for apps.

  - Transportation: Examples include HopStop, LIMOMAN, and Dublin Bus.

- *Recommended for You*: Somehow, Amazon figures out what it is that you want. I'll let you decide whether or not it makes the right choices.

Yes, there are many types of apps to choose from. If you still can't find what you are looking for, then try the search engine.

Purchasing an App on the Kindle Fire

When you find the application you are looking for, it appears as an entry (see Figure 9–4).

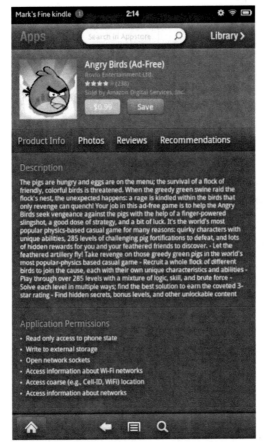 

Figure 9–4. *An entry on the Amazon Appstore for a well-known application*

You have the option to buy it or save it. Hitting the orange price button processes the payment to your Kindle Fire account, just like in the Newsstand, Books, or Videos.

Next to the purchase button is a Save button. Think of it as a bookmark for the Amazon Appstore for Android. You can access saved apps at More + in the Content menu. I will go into more detail later.

Each entry has four categories, which you can touch to learn more about the app:

- *Product Info*: The description. Also includes Application Permissions, which is required for Android Apps. This tells the user app requirements; for example, some of them require Wi-Fi.

- *Photos*: Shows screenshots from the app, which are provided by the app developer upon submission to the Amazon Appstore for Android.

- *Reviews*: Ratings by Android users (from one to five stars). You can provide your own rating if you like, along with comments.

- *Recommendations*: Apps similar to those you purchased.

The Amazon Appstore Content Bar

As you may have noticed while searching the Amazon Appstore, there is the option for selecting contents. Figure 9–5 shows it, at least at the main store.

Figure 9–5. *The Amazon Appstore content bar*

- *Categories*: Lists the categories. Acts the same as selecting the All Categories.

- *Recommended*: Tapping this button produces the same results as Recommended for You.

- *My Subscriptions*: Certain apps, such as magazines, require a subscription. They can usually be downloaded for free and viewed here (see Figure 9–6). You can change the subscription period from monthly to annual, for example, as well as turn on auto-renewal and adjust privacy preferences.

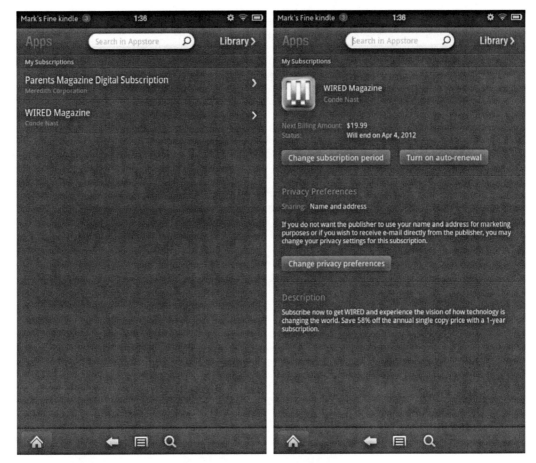

Figure 9–6. *My Subscriptions options (left) along with an individual entry (right)*

- *My Apps*. The Kindle Fire comes with several apps on the Library shelf, but they may not be installed on your system. *Pandora*, The Weather Channel, and *Words with Friends* appear in New (see Figure 9–7, left). Update Available reveals the apps that have updates (see Figure 9–7, center). All apps are listed when you tap All (see Figure 9–7, right). They can be opened or viewed in alphabetical or reverse alphabetical order by tapping the Refine button.

Figure 9–7. *My Apps options: New (left), Update Available (center), and All (right)*

■ *Settings*: This is much less complicated than other settings that I have encountered on the Kindle Fire. It has four options, which you can see in Figure 9–8.

Figure 9–8. *The Settings button on the Content menu gives only a few options.*

- *Gift Cards*: If you have received an Amazon gift card and you want to use it on apps, this is where you want to be. Tapping this opens a screen where you can enter your gift card claim code (see Figure 9–9, left) as well as view the Terms and Conditions. You can immediately apply the gift card to your account and save it for your next purchase (see Figure 9–9, right).

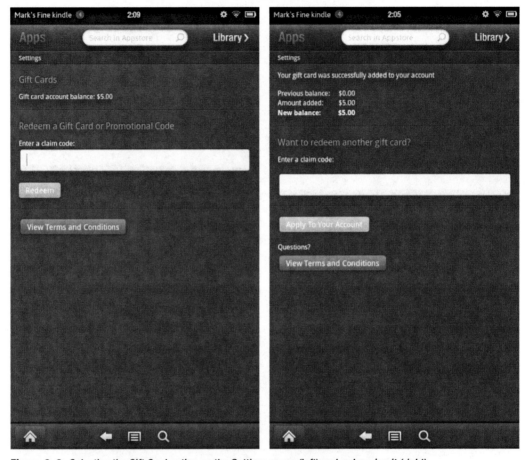

Figure 9–9. *Selecting the Gift Card option on the Settings menu (left) and redeeming it (right)*

- *Parental Controls*: I'm sure there are a lot of parents reading this book, and if you allow your children to use the Kindle Fire, then I recommend instituting the parental controls settings. Keep in mind that this is a parental control for app purchases only; you must take other precautions for areas like movies or the web. You need to tap the checkmark box to activate the parental controls (see Figure 9–10). You are required to input your password to the Amazon Market. You can then enter a four-digit pin to block anyone from entering your apps account.

Figure 9–10. *Selecting the Parental Controls on the Settings option.*

- In-App Purchasing: This allows the user to purchase digital (or, in some cases, genuine) content from the site—like newspaper subscriptions, more game levels, premium content, or extra functionality of some type. Tapping this opens a screen like the one shown in Figure 9–11. You can select or de-select the option of in-app purchases, and you need your Amazon password to check or uncheck it. If you have kids who like playing games or other apps on the Kindle Fire, I highly recommend blocking In-App purchasing. Some parents racked up large bills thanks to a child who loves to buy virtual games.

Figure 9–11. *Allowing In-App purchases*

- *Version and Release Notes*. Shows your current version.

- *More+*: Opens several categories, including the following:

    - *Saved for Later*: The Amazon Appstore has a way to bookmark a particular app just by selecting the Save option on the entry. This is where you find all your saved apps, in case you are ready to buy (see Figure 9–12).

Figure 9–12. *Apps Saved for Later*

- *Recently Viewed*: Shows the app entries that you have recently looked at, provided you viewed the entry page. Everything is arranged in a convenient list view as seen Figure 9–13. Apps open with the touch of a button. I found that unlike other shelves on the Kindle Fire, this shelf is not infinite. It shows only the last 15 apps viewed. This is why you want to use the Save option.

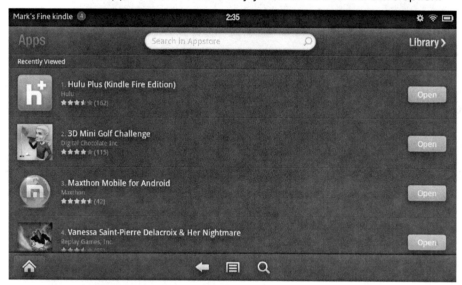

Figure 9–13. *Recently Viewed apps*

- *Contact Customer Service*: Opens a window to send an e-mail or call customer service (1-866-749–7771). If you tap the e-mail button that you see in Figure 9–14, you are given a list of the type of e-mail that you want to send, depending on the number of e-mail accounts you have on your Kindle Fire. This is not the only way to contact the company; you can also go to Quick Setting ➤ Help & Feedback ➤ Contact Customer Service ➤ Apps. (See Chapter 2 for more information.)

Figure 9–14. *Contacting customer service through e-mail or by phone*

■ *Leave Feedback*: Believe it or not, this allows you to give the Appstore a rating of 1 through 5 stars. You can also generalize your feedback with Recommendation, Bug, and Comment (see Figure 9–15).

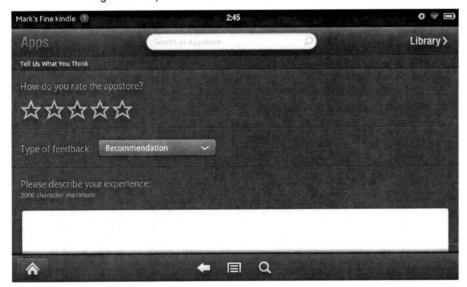

Figure 9–15. *Rating the Amazon Appstore*

■ *Help*: Offers help from the Amazon Appstore for Android. I recommended checking it out (see Figure 9–16.) If your particular question isn't addressed here, go to Help & Feedback in Quick Settings.

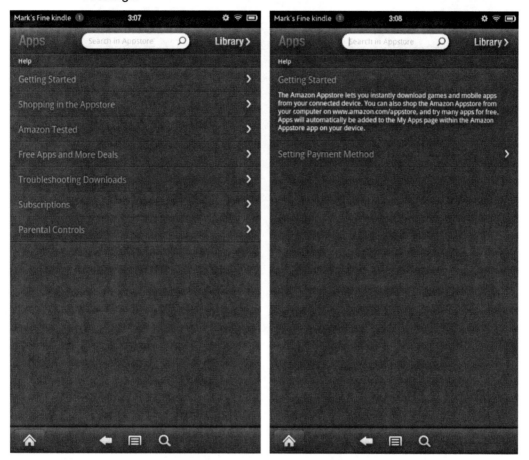

Figure 9–16. *The Help section on the Contents menu*

■ *Legal*: Features the terms of use, privacy policy and terms and conditions for gift cards.

Removing an App

There are three ways to remove an application from the Apps shelf. The first and easiest way is to go to the Apps Library and simply press and hold the app icon, and you are given a chance to Add to Favorites or Remove from Device (see Figure 9–17).

Figure 9–17. *Touching and holding an app in the Library*

Certain apps—such as Gallery, Facebook, Contacts, and e-mail—cannot be removed. I guess those are programs are critical to the system and shouldn't be deleted.

A second, more complicated method of app removal requires following these steps:

1. Tap the cog wheel icon to open Quick Settings.

2. Tap More+.

3. Scroll down and tap Applications.

4. Tap Filter By and select Running Applications, Third Party Applications, and All Applications. You will find only certain apps on the first two categories, but the one you want to remove should be there.

5. Tap the app you want to remove. You will see a screen that looks similar to Figure 9–18.

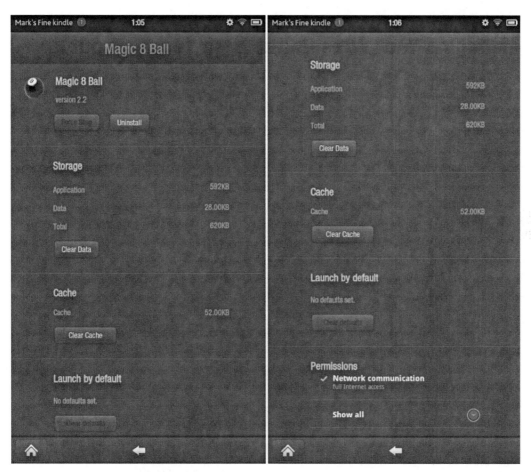

Figure 9–18. *Viewing an app in Quick Settings*

6. Storage shows the amount of data and cache the app takes up. It also gives the Permissions required for the program. Tap Uninstall to remove the app.

A third way of removing apps is connected to managing your online account.

Apps

Managing Your Apps Online from Your Computer

Like other apps, you can manage your favorite apps from your online account at
www.amazon.com/manageyoursubscriptions. Click Your **Apps and Devices** ➤ **Manage your**
Apps. You should see a screen similar to Figure 9–19.

Figure 9–19. *Managing your Apps online*

There is an Actions button at the end of each app. In this menu, you will find the
following options:

- *Review this App*: Allows you to rate the app online.

- *View Order Details*: A virtual receipt for your app.

- *Your In-App Items*: Keeps track of the in-app items you have
purchased.

- *Delete this App*: Yet another way to remove an app from your App
shelf.

Buying an App Online for Your Kindle Fire

If you want to buy an app on your Kindle Fire while you're anywhere online, this is easy. For example, I went to Amazon.com and searched for the paid version of *Where's My Water*. My entry page on Amazon.com is seen in Figure 9–20.

Figure 9–20. *Buying an app online on the Amazon Appstore*

I can purchase it easily with the 1-Click button to the right. This entry is set to go with my Kindle Fire as well as my Motorola Droid X. This is because I own two Android devices. However, I only want this app for my Kindle Fire. *Where's My Water* won't be charged to my Droid X unless I go to the Android Market on that device and run another transaction. After making the app purchase for my Kindle Fire, I see a screen like the one shown in Figure 9–21.

Figure 9–21. *I purchased an app for my Kindle Fire*

As you can from the message in green on the right, there is still more to do, but the purchase transacted and I get the receipt via e-mail. The app isn't on my device until I install it, however. So, I go to the Contents button on my Kindle Fire and select My Apps. I see a list of apps that have been downloaded. All I have to do is tap Install.

The Appstore for Android also has categories for its apps, as follows:

- *Best Sellers*: Shows the Top 100 Paid and the Top 100 Free, and bestselling categories.

- *Deals*: Features the app deals of the day.

- *New Releases*: Features the latest apps.

- *Test Drive Apps*: A try-before-you-buy feature.

- *Shop Android Phones*: Takes you to the market to buy an Android phone.

- *Your Apps and Devices*: The screen you want to use for sorting through your apps.

- *Getting Started*: For first-time Amazon Android user who hasn't yet connected to his smartphone.

- *Help*: Offers app support and assistance. Several questions are answered here, as seen in Figure 9–22.

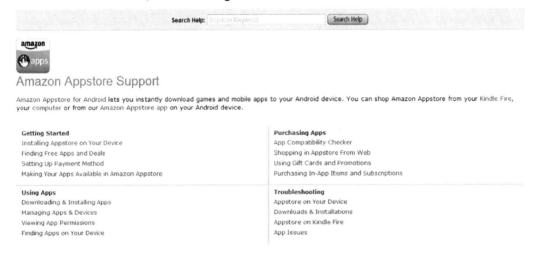

Figure 9–22. *Amazon Appstore support*

Summary

Even though the apps available for the Kindle Fire are limited to the Amazon Appstore for Android, their selection is very diverse and growing daily. Purchasing an app is made simple with one-touch purchasing. Apps are grouped in distinct categories to make browsing easier as well.

The Kindle Fire user has the option of bookmarking an app that she is considering. Other options include gift card redemption, parental controls, and in-app purchasing.

There are several ways to remove an app from your Apps shelf; one is by managing them online. Apps can also be downloaded to the Kindle Fire.

Chapter 10

Web

It is hard to believe that we were still using dial-up internet about a decade ago, and it has only been a few years since we were able to get the internet on our mobile devices. These are technologies that I now cannot live without.

In all honesty, I admit that I usually don't surf the web on a mobile device. I'm a Generation Xer that had to adapt to the web after college. I was not raised on it like the kids who were born shortly after me. The simple truth is that I use the web best when I am at a desktop or on a laptop, with a mouse and the clickity-click of a keyboard in front of me. I've tried using the web from my smartphone, and I found the screen too constricting, the touchscreen keyboard nothing short of annoying. I also found the speed of the mobile web to be much slower compared to broadband.

Fortunately, the web on the Kindle Fire is an entirely different experience: the screen is big enough for me to see what I need to see (including video), the keyboard is easier to use, and it uses the Silk web browser.

Silk is powered by Amazon's Web Services (AWS). According to the *Kindle Fire User's Guide*, it "couples the capabilities and interactivity of your Kindle Fire with the massive computing power, memory, and network connectivity of Amazon's cloud." This is different than most browsers, which still use the same basic architecture based on browsers of the nineties. Whenever you load a web site, you are essentially requesting information from a certain place, then it gets information from you, and this constant trade-off of subsystems is the reason why many web pages don't load as fast as you would like. Amazon developed "split architecture" that is in play every time a web page is loaded. Silk makes a decision about which of the subsystems are run locally and which execute remotely, using the Kindle Fire device and the cloud together for a faster web surfing experience.

Silk is a simple interface for surfing the web (see Figure 10–1, left), accessible by tapping Web on the Home screen. Like later versions of Microsoft's Internet Explorer, Google's Chrome, and Mozilla's Firefox, it uses tabbed browsing.

Tapping the plus sign (+) in the upper-right corner opens a new tab/screen. This also displays your most visited pages as thumbnails (see Figure 10–2, right); tapping a thumbnail opens the page.

 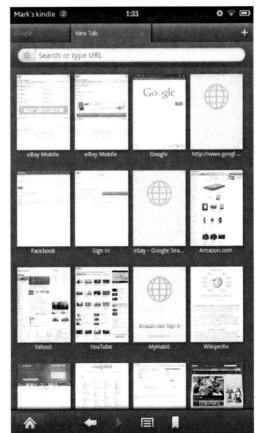

Figure 10–1. *Surfing the web on a Kindle Fire*

The screen orientation feature for the Kindle Fire works advantageously in the Web category. Personally, I prefer using the Web in landscape format because it makes it feel more like a desktop or laptop where the browser screen is wider than it is tall. The typeface is also slightly larger (see Figure 10–2).

Figure 10–2. *The Web in landscape format*

I already discussed how to connect to a wireless access point. I don't think that I need to talk about how to enter a URL. In case you need a reminder, just type it in and tap Go. Yes, this is pretty basic. The only thing that I really need to bring up at this point is how to close the tabs. All that is required is touching the X in the right-hand corner of the tabs.

If you have done any work on iOS browsers, like those on the iPad, iPhone, and iPod Touch, then you are probably familiar with pinch-to-zoom to get a close-up view of a web site. The Kindle Fire has a pinch-to-zoom feature that works just as well.

Another thing that might interest you is that you can download an image on pages with picture files on them. Simply press and hold the image, and you are given the option to Save Image or View Image (see Figure 10–3, left). When you save the image, it becomes available in your Downloads folder, which I will explain later in this chapter. As for viewing the image, it is placed on a blank screen (see Figure 10–3, right).

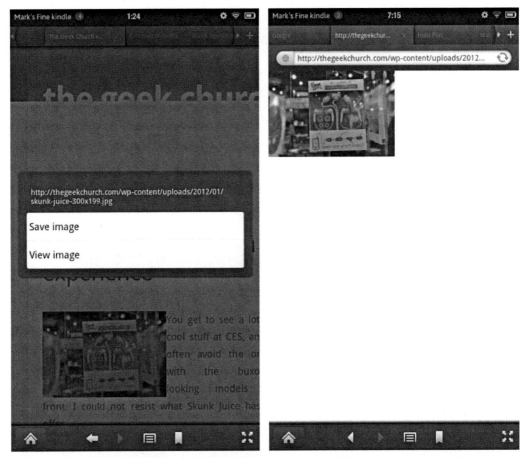

Figure 10–3. *Pressing and holding an image on the Silk browser gives you two options (left); choosing Save puts it in Kindle Fire memory, choosing View puts the image on a blank screen (right).*

Another feature worth noting is that you have the option of highlighting text and copying it to a clipboard. It is a slightly different process of highlighting than with Newsstand and Books. All you need to do is touch and hold a word; you get a highlighted area surrounded by two trapezoidal-shaped brackets (see Figure 10–4), which can be pressed and held in either direction to highlight more text. Once you are done highlighting, tap the highlighted area, and the text is instantly copied to the clipboard, where you can paste it into another document later.

Figure 10–4. *Highlighting in the Kindle Fire's Web*

Menu Bar for the Web

The bottom menu bar is quite different than other categories on the Kindle Fire, and it changes often.

Going Back and Forward

You usually see the Back button (see Figure 10–5). Tapping it enough times sends you back to the Home screen.

Figure 10–5. *The bottom menu bar on the Kindle Fire, with the Back button as an arrow shape*

Sometimes the Back button changes shape, and appears like it does in Figure 10–6. Here, the Back and Forward buttons appear as they do when you navigate on a computer browser.

Figure 10–6. *The Kindle Fire's Web menu bar with the Back and Forward keys as triangular shapes*

Bookmarks

Before I get to the Contents button, I want to discuss Bookmarks (see Figure 10–7). If you are on a site that you want to bookmark, tap the bookmark icon located on the right of the bottom menu bar. As you can see in Figure 10–7, your bookmarks are available in two views, grid view and list view. Just tap either of the two buttons in the upper-right corner.

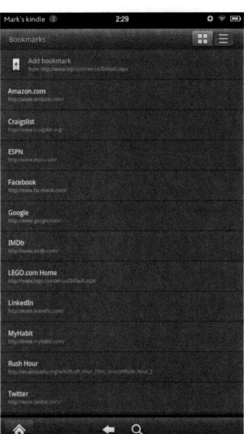

Figure 10–7. *The Bookmarks page, in list view (left) and grid view (right)*

When you hit the Bookmarks button, the web site that you were previously viewing is immediately placed in the upper-left corner as a new bookmark, with a giant plus (+) symbol on it and a caption reading Bookmark Archived (see Figure 10–7, left). If you touch that particular icon, you are given the option of adding that bookmark with a name and location, as seen in Figure 10–8.

Figure 10–8. *The option to add a bookmark*

If you tap one of the other bookmarks, in any mode, you get a menu like the one shown in Figure 10–9.

Figure 10–9. *Bookmark menu options*

The Bookmark menu options include the following:

- *Open*: Opens a bookmarked web site in the current open tab.

- *Open in New Tab*: Opens the web site in a separate tab, which is helpful for when you want to view multiple sites.

- *Open in Background Tab*: Opens a tab with the web site in the background. As you might have guessed, this can create quite a crowd of tabs.

- *Share Link*: Opens way to share the site with friends. A selection box like the one shown in Figure 10–10 shows what you can use to share your link. I believe that Facebook and e-mail are the defaults, but if your friends have similar applications installed, like Evernote, you have that option as well.

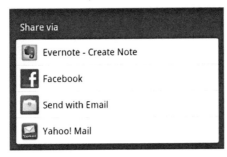

Figure 10–10. *E-mail options in sharing a link*

- *Copy Link URL*: Copies the URL to a clipboard so that you can paste it elsewhere.

- *Edit Bookmark*: Allows the user to change the name of the bookmark or the URL. Tapping this opens a window similar to Figure 10–8. You can edit the name and location from there.

- *Delete*: Removes the site from Bookmarks.

Full Screen

To the far right on the menu bar is an arrow explosion; this is the full screen mode. Full screen gives your web site a little more real estate than the menu bar and tabs allow (see Figure 10–11). Full screen is removed by finger swiping up the bottom center area.

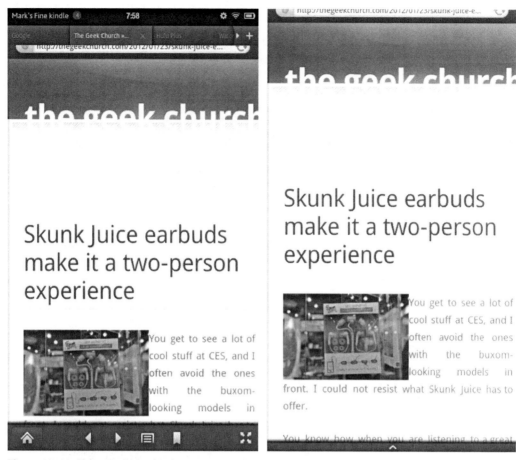

Figure 10–11. *Using the Web with the menu bar (left) and the full screen function (right)*

Contents Menu

The Contents menu can do quite a lot. It offers six choices at the touch of a button (see Figure 10–12).

Figure 10–12. *The Contents menu for Web*

These functions include the following:

- *Add Bookmark*: Allows the user to set a web site as a bookmark; opens a window like the one shown in Figure 10–8.

- *Share Page*: Acts the same as Share Link on the Bookmark page, with the same option window as seen in Figure 10–10.

- *Find in Page*: Allows you to find a specific word or phrase on a web page (see Figure 10–13). To do this, simply type the first few letters of the word you are searching.

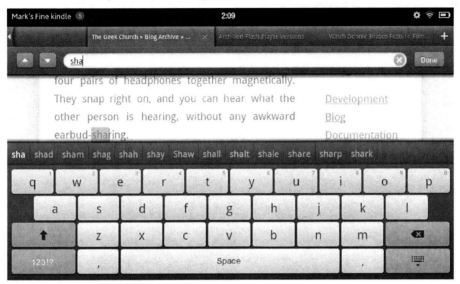

Figure 10–13. *Find in Page performs text searches*

- *History*: Places your Silk browsing history on one page (see Figure 10–14, left). More History is available by tapping Last 7 Days (see Figure 10–14, right). Clear All deletes your history. By the way, tapping the bookmark icon to the right side of each entry adds the site to Bookmarks.

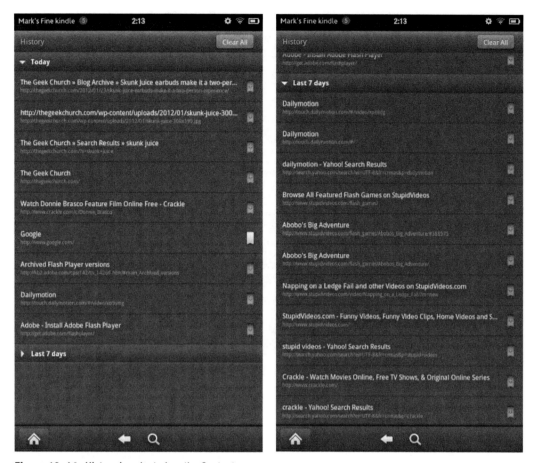

Figure 10–14. *History is selected on the Contents menu*

■ *Downloads*: Earlier in this chapter, I discussed that a Web user can download images from the browser. Other files can be downloaded as well. Anything that you download from the Web on the Kindle Fire is found here (see Figure 10–15). Accessing downloads is as easy. A check box to the left of each file allows you to delete the download (or uncheck to delete with the Clear Selection option). Tapping the Contents button in the middle of this page gives the option to sort the files by size.

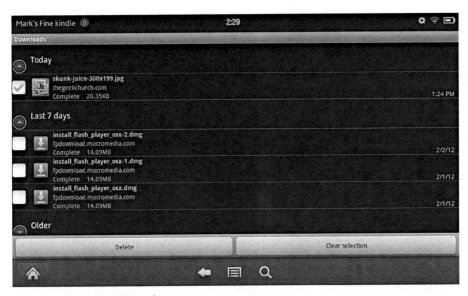

Figure 10–15. *Downloads section*

- Settings: Provides several functions; so much that I want to devote quite a bit of this chapter to it. See Figure 10–16 to view everything at a glance.

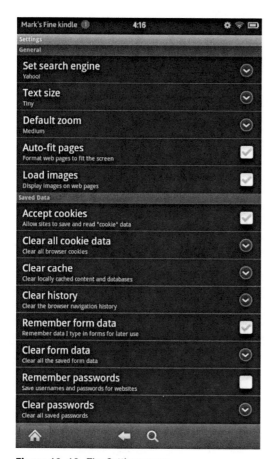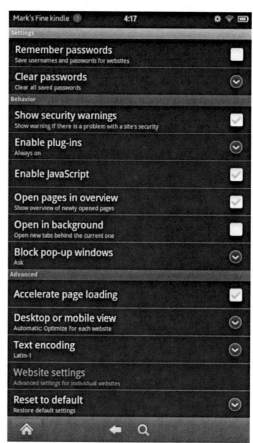

Figure 10–16. *The Settings menu*

■ *Set Search Engine*: Opens a window that allows you to set a default search engine from three choices: Google, Bing, and Yahoo.

■ *Text Size*: Adjusts the browser text size. Options include tiny, small, normal, large, and huge. Figure 10–17 shows the difference between tiny and huge.

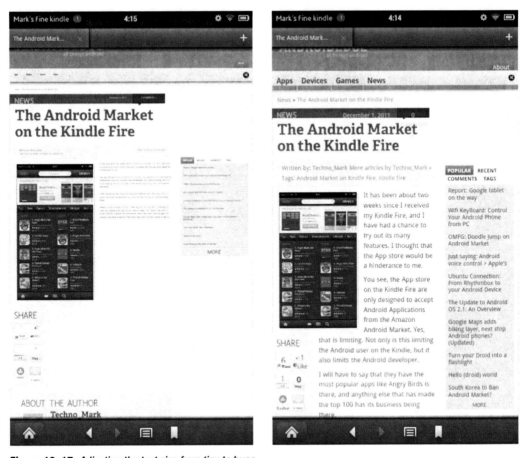

Figure 10–17. *Adjusting the text size from tiny to huge*

- *Default Zoom*: Offers three zooming selections: far, medium, and close. The differences are clear (see Figure 10–18).

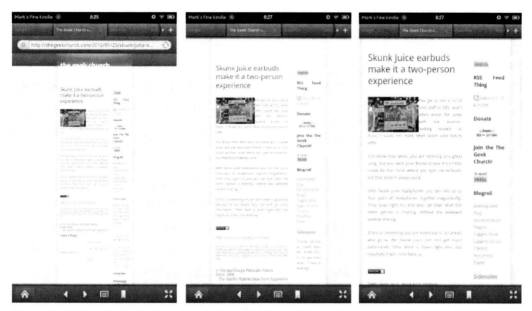

Figure 10–18. *Zooming far (left), medium (center), and close (right)*

- *Auto-fit Pages*: Formats web pages to fit on the screen. I find this really works best when switching screen orientation.

- *Load Images*: Prevents images from showing. I am not certain why you would want images disabled. A before and after is shown in Figure 10–19.

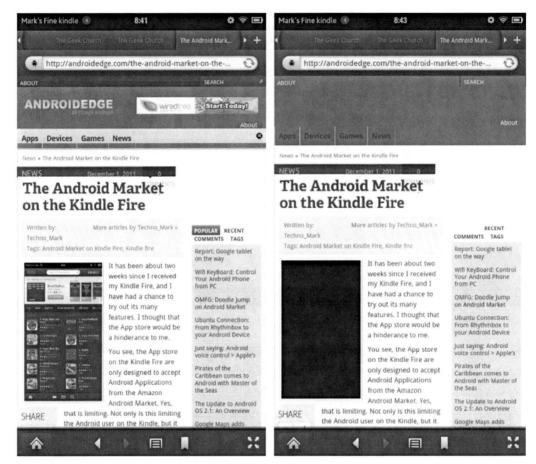

Figure 10–19. *Load Images completely removes the images from web sites.*

- *Accept Cookies*: Allows a site to save and read cookie data. For those who don't know what cookies are, it is used for an origin web site to send state information to a user's browser and for the browser to return the information to the origin site. I think people associate cookies with something bad, but they can't be programmed, carry viruses, and can't install malware on the host computer. They could possibly be used by spyware to track a user's activities.

- *Clear All Cookie Data*: Clears all the cookie data.

- *Clear Cache*: A cache is a component that can store data so future requests of the data will show up faster. Have you ever noticed that web sites that you have visited before come up faster? This was even true even with dial-up. This can be a problem when the web site design changes because sometimes the site tries to load the old cache. If you tap Clear Cache, it should resolve this problem.

- *Clear History*: Loading a new tab automatically gives you a grid view of previously visited sites. If you don't want other users of you Kindle Fire to see what sites you viewed, then you can hit this to clear them out.

- *Remember Form Data*: You may have noticed that when you fill out online web forms, you find your data already there. This is form data.

- *Clear Form Data*: In case you have form data that you want to be cleared, this is where to do it.

- *Remember Passwords*: There are two types of people in the world: those who always want their computer to remember their passwords and those that are constantly worried about security and always type passwords. Personally, I don't like the idea of anyone getting a hold of my Kindle Fire and breaking into files over the internet, which is why I turned off this feature. There are other ways to prevent data theft if you are worried about it, though.

- *Clear Passwords*: If you do not like having a browser that remembers your passwords, you can clear them out here.

- *Show Security Warnings*: If you have virus protection programs on your laptop or desktop, then you are well aware of occasional security warnings that occur when you are trying to do something online that your protection program doesn't like. If you don't want to see these occasional warnings, then you can hit this and be relieved of them.

- *Enable Flash*. Unlike the iPad, the Kindle Fire uses the Adobe Flash Player quite well for video viewing. If you are having trouble viewing videos, you should check here to see if your Enable Flash is on. You can also disable it here.

- *Enable Plug-ins*: For some programs, you need a set of software components designed to key in a larger application. For example, video programs like Crackle and YouTube run very well on the Web browser. This is because the Adobe program helps stream the video.

- *Enable JavaScript*: If you are the type that wants to turn off the JavaScript because you don't like the idea of that being a point of security holes, you can disable JavaScript here.

- *Open Pages in Overview*: When this is selected, you see the web sites just like you would on your computer browser.

- *Open in Background*: Designed to open new tabs behind the current one.

- *Block Pop-up Windows*: If you don't like pop-up windows, you want to access this. You have three options: Ask (asks if you want to see a pop-up), Never (completely blocks them from occurring), and Always (allows the pop-up windows).

- *Accelerate Page Loading*: The Silk browser has split-level architecture that use the cloud and the device to surf the web. Unchecking this option means surfing directly to web sites without offloading some of the processing through Amazon's servers.

- *Desktop or Mobile* View: Some web sites offer a mobile view. Mobile views are usually simpler than the regular desktop view. You can automatically optimize for each web site, desktop, and mobile.

- *Text Encoding*: If you want to change your text encoding from the default Latin-1 (ISO-8859-1), this is where you would do that.

- *Web Site Settings*: Advanced settings, which covers individual sites.

- *Reset to Default*: Reverts to default settings for the Web.

Other Browsers for the Kindle Fire

When the iPhone's Safari became a popular web-browsing tool, a lot of other companies created iOS apps for web browsing. Two of the more popular apps are Dolphin and Opera Mini.

A search for "Web Browser for Kindle Fire" on the Amazon Appstore for Android didn't reveal much. I found an app called Maxthon Mobile (see Figure 10–20, right), but not many others (see Figure 10–20, left).

I tried out Maxthon; it has a very different type of menu than Silk. I'll let you try it out for yourself if you are curious. Just know that when you have Maxthon on your system, the Kindle Fire will always ask what browser you want to use before it opens a web site.

Keep your eyes peeled for new web browsers for the Kindle Fire, but don't be surprised if you don't ever find many others. Amazon might want a web browser monopoly with Silk, and may not green-light other competitors into the browser market.

Figure 10–20. *A search for "web browser for Kindle Fire" revealed a small list (left), with Maxthon at the top.*

Summary

As long as the Kindle Fire is synced wirelessly, the user has access to the web via the Silk browser. Data speed is pretty quick. The Silk browser is a lot like other browsers made for laptops and desktops; it features tabs and bookmarks.

The Web category features pinch-to-zoom, downloads, and highlighting text. The menu bar has several options, including back, forward, bookmarks, full screen, and a Contents menu so that you can truly customize your internet experience on the Kindle Fire.

So far, there are not a lot of other web browser apps available for the Kindle Fire, but you might want to occasionally check the Amazon Appstore for Android to see if that changes.

Chapter 11

E-mail

While there isn't a way to connect a Kindle Fire to cellular phone network as yet, you can still do a lot on it, provided you are connected to a Wi-Fi network. If you are like me, you spend a significant portion of the day checking and answering e-mail. I discovered that a lot of e-mail tasks can be done during the "downtime" between projects.

For example, if you are at a train station or a bus stop with a Wi-Fi access point, you might as well use the time to handle your e-mail business before you arrive at the office. This is assuming that you are not reading books, newspapers, magazines, watching video, or doing anything else on your Kindle Fire. Considering that some activities can be done offline, you should take advantage of your e-mail whenever you are at station or stop with a Wi-Fi access point; do your offline activities on the train or bus.

The Kindle Fire allows you to check and respond to e-mail. It also allows for organization so your inbox does not get cluttered. You can check multiple accounts at once, as well as open attachments.

Setting Up Your E-Mail Account for Yahoo! Mail Using the Web Browser

I found that there are several ways of looking at e-mail on the Kindle Fire. If you use a web-based e-mail system, you could use a web browser, just like you would on your computer.

For example, if you have a Yahoo! account that you want to access, you can go to www.yahoo.com and click Mail. Trying to access your e-mail this way might lead to a screen that looks like Figure 11–1. The reason why I say "might" is because some Kindle Fire users have reported that they don't see this screen; you might see a screen that looks like the opening e-mail screen on a computer browser.

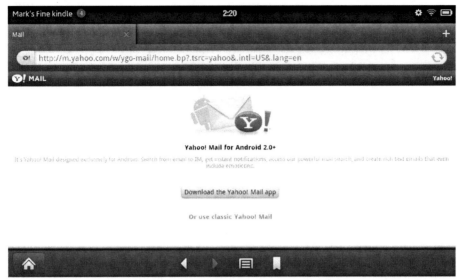

Figure 11–1. *Some users experience this screen when opening Yahoo! Mail on the Kindle Fire.*

The Kindle offers users access to the Yahoo! Mail app. You could also use the classic Yahoo! Mail if you prefer your experience to be just like that on your desktop or laptop.

If you want to download the Yahoo! Mail app for the Kindle Fire, just tap the button. After it downloads, enter your Yahoo! ID and password. Next, you see a screen like that shown in Figure 11–2.

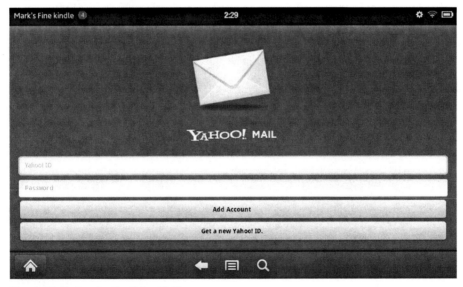

Figure 11–2. *Opening the Yahoo Mail! app*

Of course, you might not have a Yahoo! e-mail account. The Kindle Fire allows you to view your e-mail from many different accounts, in one place.

The Kindle Fire's E-mail App

In the Apps page you find an app marked E-mail. Tap it, and you should see a screen like the one shown in Figure 11–3.

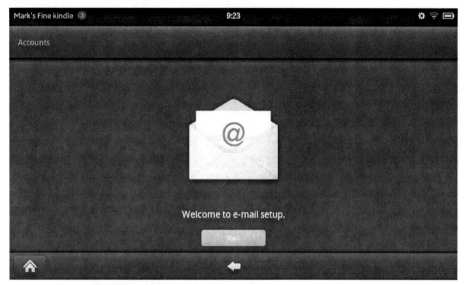

Figure 11–3. *The E-mail app set-up on the Kindle Fire*

Next, you are asked to select from a list of potential e-mail providers (see Figure 11–4, left). You select from Gmail, Yahoo!, Hotmail, AOL, or another provider when you tap Other.

You need your login information for the account, including the password (see Figure 11–4, center). Check Show Password if you want to see the actual characters typed out, instead of the series of dots that you normally see.

When you enter your login information, you are asked to type the name that will appear on outgoing messages (see Figure 11–4, right). Finally, you are asked to give the account a name, but this is completely optional.

You can select this as your default e-mail by tapping the check box. You can always change it later if you want, as I will explain.

Your contacts are automatically put into place in the Contacts app if you check Import Contacts.

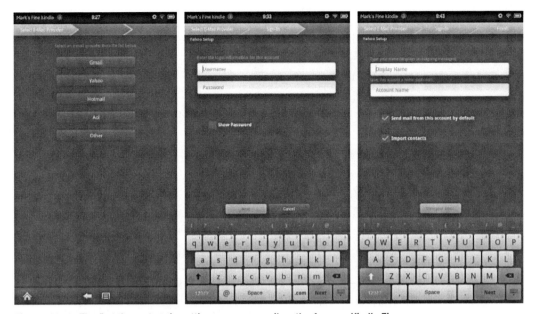

Figure 11–4. *The first three steps in setting up your e-mail on the Amazon Kindle Fire*

Once your e-mail account is set up, you should see an e-mail browser similar to the one shown in Figure 11–5. The unified inbox lists your e-mail accounts. I explain how to set up a new e-mail account shortly.

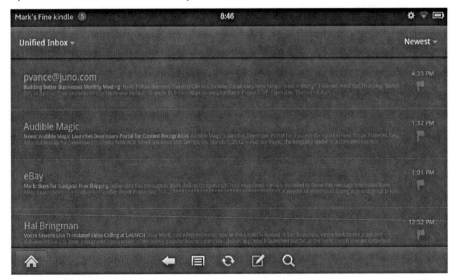

Figure 11–5. *Your e-mail inbox*

The Newest drop-down menu on the right lists about 30 of your most recent e-mails. You can also sort e-mail by the following:

- *Oldest*: Lists the oldest e-mail first, but only 30 are available for viewing.

- *Subject*: Sorts all e-mail alphabetically by subject, starting with numerals.

- *Sender*: Sorts e-mail alphabetically by the sender's first name.

- *Flagged*: Flagged e-mail lists first. To flag an e-mail, tap the flag icon next to the e-mail message.

- *Read*: Sorts e-mail that was read by date.

- *Unread*: Sorts e-mail that is not read to appear first.

- *Attachments*: Any e-mails with attachments appear first, starting with the most recent.

After reading, if you want to do something further with an e-mail, press and hold it for a list of choices (see Figure 11–6).

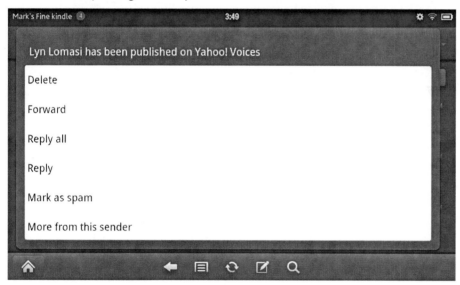

Figure 11–6. *The choices for editing your e-mail*

Your options include the following:

- *Delete*: Removes the e-mail message.

- *Forward*: Sends the message to another person by entering another e-mail address in Send To.

- *Reply All*: If you receive an e-mail that was also sent to others, this is a way to reply to the original sender as well as the others.

- *Reply*: Replies to the original sender.

- *Mark as Spam*: Marks an e-mail message as spam, thus training the spam filter to flag similar messages as spam.

- *More from This Sender*: Lists other e-mail messages by a particular sender.

The menu bar at the bottom of Figure 11–6 is different than most menu bars. For example, here the first button is the Back button.

The Refresh button has an icon that looks like a circle. This is a good way to make certain that you have your latest e-mail messages.

The search engine is designed to search e-mail messages. It works just like any other search engine function; it is good for searching for a particular message by sender or subject.

The Contents Button

The Contents button on the menu bar has many options, including the following:

- *Edit List*: A check box that opens a list of options. Tap Done when you are finished. Each message has an option to flag by tapping the flag icon (see Figure 11–7).

  - *Mark as Unread*: Messages that you want to stand out after reading them.

  - *Move*: Allows you to send checked e-mails to different folder, including Drafts, Sent, Trash, and any other folders set up on your e-mail account.

  - *Delete*: Removes the e-mail message.

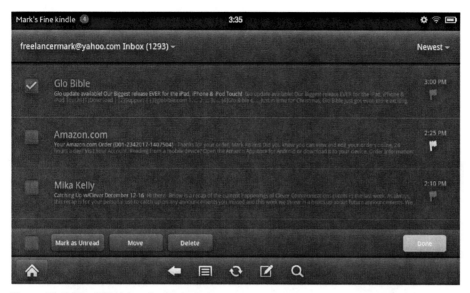

Figure 11–7. *The Edit List on the Contents menu*

- *Help & Feedback*: Brings you to the same page that you find in Settings in the upper-right corner, along with the Help option.

- *Contacts*: Lists your contacts, which are automatically uploaded when you set up your account. I go into more detail later in this chapter, but Figure 11–8 shows how it is organized alphabetically.

Figure 11–8. *The Contacts list on Kindle Fire's e-mail, also accessible on the Contacts App*

- *Accounts*: The place to go if you want more than one e-mail account on your Kindle Fire. Tapping the Contents button here, provides the following options:

    - *Contacts*: Takes you to the Contacts page.

    - *Add Account*: Sets up additional accounts. Tap the left corner to switch between e-mail accounts. The numbers after the e-mail addresses refer to the number of e-mails that have not been read (see Figure 11–9).

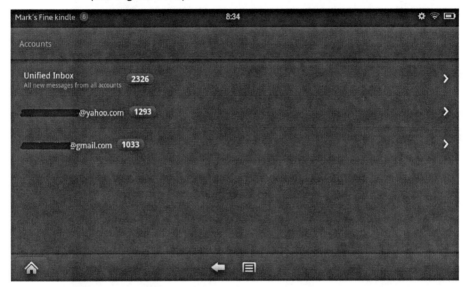

Figure 11–9. *Select an e-mail account*

- *Settings*: Enable Debug Logging allows you to log extra diagnostic information; Log Sensitive Information shows passwords in logs(see Figure 11–10).

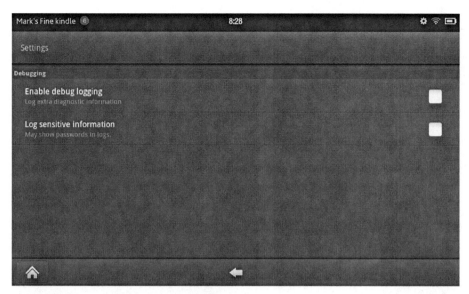

Figure 11–10. *The settings menu for Accounts*

■ *Folders*: Displays all the folders available in your e-mail account, such as the Inbox, Sent, Spam, Drafts, Trash, any folders that you created. There is a Contents button here that provides the following three options:

■ *Empty Trash*: A clean sweep of deleted e-mails.

■ *Accounts*: Yet another way of switching to accounts.

■ *Settings*: Acts the same as Settings previously discussed.

■ *Settings*: Like most Settings menus, there are quite a lot of options available (see Figure 11–11).

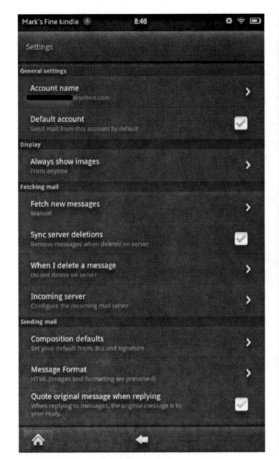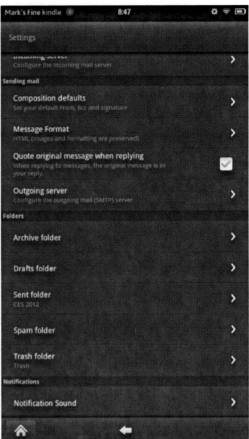

Figure 11–11. *The settings menu for e-mail*

These options include the following:

- *Account Name*: Allows you to enter the e-mail account that you want to access. It is probably much easier to simply go to any e-mail's main page, select the upper-left corner, and pick the e-mail account that you want.

- *Default Account*: If you check this, then the e-mail account that you entered in the Account Name becomes the default account.

- *Always Show Images*: Provides the option of blocking certain images from select people, as shown in Figure 11–12. You have the option of tapping No to block the images. From Contacts shows only the images from your contact list. From Anyone shows images from anyone.

Figure 11–12. *The Always Show Images feature*

> ▨ *Fetch New Messages*: Choose to get your messages from Push or Manual.

> ▨ *Sync Server Deletions*: Removes messages deleted on the server.

> ▨ *When I Delete a Message*: Opens the options shown in Figure 11–13.

Figure 11–13. *The options for the When I Delete a Message feature*

- *Incoming Server*: Configures the incoming server settings, in case you need to do it manually.

- *Message Composition Options*: Provides options for your messages (see Figure 11–14). For example, your name, the e-mail address, and an automatic Bcc (a blind carbon copy of the message is sent to others). You can also add a signature, which is a line of text at the end of an e-mail message; it defaults as "Sent from my Kindle Fire".

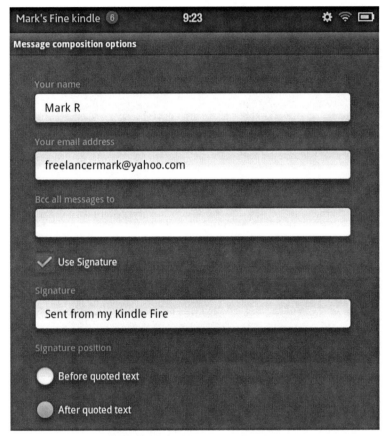

Figure 11–14. *Message Composition Options for e-mail*

- *Message Format*: Formats e-mail messages as plain text, which removes images and formatting, and HTML, where images and formatting are preserved (see Figure 11–15).

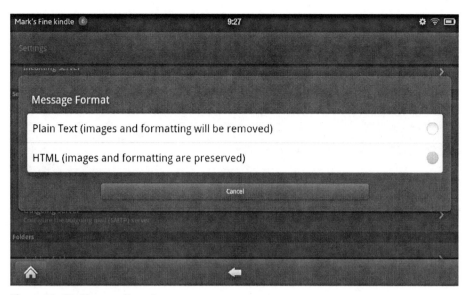

Figure 11–15. *Message Format*

- *Quote Original Message When Replying*: Provides the original message to in a reply.

- *Outgoing Server Settings*: I personally don't mess with the settings of my outgoing server, but if you are the type, then this will be helpful for you. You will probably only need to adjust these settings if your e-mail provider is not among those in the Kindle Fire (see Figure 11–4, left).

- *Folders*: Access content in your Archive, Drafts, Sent, Spam, Trash, and other folders.

- *Notification Sound*: Hear a sound whenever a new e-mail comes in; similar to the notification sounds discussed in Chapter 2.

Composing a New Message

The paper and pencil button on the menu bar is for writing a new message. You also have the option to add an Attachment. You have the option of sending a message right away, or saving it as a draft to complete and send later (see Figure 11–16).

Figure 11–16. *A new message in Kindle Fire e-mail*

Opening an Attachment

If you receive a message with an attachment, you have the option to open or save it (see Figure 11–17).

Figure 11–17. *Opening an attachment*

Tapping Open gives you the option to select which program to open. This depends on the type of file the attachment is. In Figure 11–17, the attachment is a PDF, which opens in Amazon Kindle or Quickoffice Pro.

Tapping the Save button automatically downloads the attachment, which can be opened later. You will get a quick note that will appear on screen showing where the save location is. Make certain to remember it for latere.

Contacts

You can download your contacts from whatever e-mail program you use. Your Contacts list looks like the one shown in Figure 11–8.

Navigation is pretty simple with scrolling/finger swipes. A proper name is found by touching the alphabetical list on the side. By pressing and holding, you access a few options (see Figure 11–18).

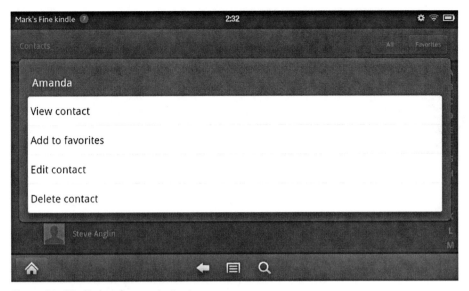

Figure 11–18. *Choices for a contact entry*

- *View Contact*: Displays contact information.

- *Add to Favorites*: You have the option of viewing all your contacts or just the favorites. This is one way that you can determine whether your contact is a favorite.

- *Edit Contact*: Allows you to edit information.

- *Delete Contact*: Deletes a contact, at least from the Kindle Fire Contacts application.

- *Send E-mail to*: Send an e-mail to a particular address. This feature also asks you what e-mail program you want to use.

The Contacts App Contents Menu

Tapping Contents on the bottom menu bar provides three options: New Contact, Settings, and Import/Export.

New Contact

As you can see in Figure 11–19, you can add all pertinent information about your new contact.

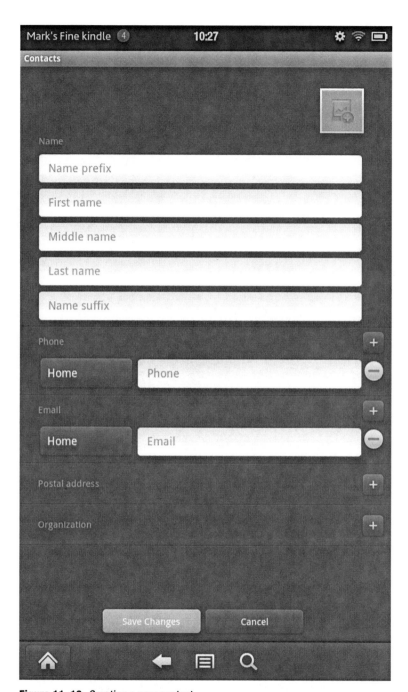

Figure 11–19. *Creating a new contact*

There are several categories. The first is Name, which includes the following:

■ Name prefix

- First name
- Middle name
- Last name
- Name suffix

It gets very interesting when you get to Phone. You will notice the plus sign on the right. This creates another area to type in a phone number. Choose from many categories, including the following:

- Home
- Mobile
- Work
- Work Fax
- Home Fax
- Pager
- Other
- Custom
- Callback
- Car
- Company Main
- ISDN
- Main
- Other Fax
- Radio
- Telex
- TTY TDD
- Work Mobile
- Work Pager
- Assistant
- MMS

Custom allows you enter in your own particular label. If you don't need the number anymore, you can remove it by touching the minus sign tab.

E-mail offers a selection similar to the phone number, but you can only choose from the following labels:

- Home

- Work

- Other

- Mobile

- Custom

The Postal Address also offers options for labels, as follows:

- Street

- PO box

- City

- State

- ZIP Code

- Country

Organization allows you to select a company name and a title, and select from the following labels:

- Work

- Other

- Custom

The Contents menu can also do the following:

- Done

- Revert

- Delete Contact

- Join

Uploading a Picture of a Contact

In the upper-right corner of a new contact screen is a small, gray square. This is the space to upload a picture of your contact. Tap it and you are taken to your Gallery.

The Kindle Fire has no camera, so you have to upload the picture to your Gallery or any other place on your Kindle Fire that stores photos. This can be done from the Documents section or by connecting your computer via USB.

Settings

There are only two options in Settings, as you can see in Figure 11–20.

Figure 11–20. *The Settings menu on the Contacts screen*

They have two features: Sort List By, which sorts by first name or last name, and Import/Export Contacts, which allows you to pull in or send out contact information.

Summary

If you are in a Wi-Fi hot spot, you might as well take the time to check your e-mail on the Kindle Fire. Setting up can be done on the web. Some e-mail providers, like Yahoo!, have an app for e-mail.

The Kindle Fire has an e-mail app. The setup is simple and can be used for multiple accounts. E-mails can be sorted in various ways and editing them is easy. There are various settings on the e-mail that provide more customization for the Kindle Fire e-mail user; you can even open attachments.

The Kindle Fire e-mail attachment imports the user's e-mail contacts. You can edit contact information and even add a picture.

All in all, the Kindle Fire really is just like using a mobile phone to check and respond to e-mail, but with a slightly larger screen. I recommend using it for e-mail when a computer is not available.

Chapter 12

Social Networking

It is hard to believe that we have lived in a world that has only had social networking sites like Facebook and Twitter for less than a decade. I'm sure that some of us wonder how we lived without social networking sites; and then there are others of us who don't really care about it at all.

Sure, there is the percentage that will never embrace social networking, but one cannot argue that sites like Facebook and Twitter aren't a part of today's culture. In all honesty, I can't think of a faster way to get to know what people are up to; it has really changed the way we relate with one another.

I'm sure that we all have more Facebook friends than we can handle. We can look at all their updates, pictures, and timelines at our leisure. Think about how today's news has been affected by Twitter, like when it floods with tweets about social unrest.

Like e-mail, the Kindle Fire is a way to keep up with our social networking life, provided you are close to a Wi-Fi a hot spot. If you are at a coffee house or library and have some time to kill, you may as well check social networking sites like Facebook, Twitter, LinkedIn, and Google+.

Facebook

Those who want to Facebook on the Kindle Fire can. Simply tap the Facebook app that is already in your Favorites list by default. The fact that the Facebook appears in Favorites shows that Amazon knew that Kindle Fire users would use the tablet to access the number-one social networking site.

Tapping the Facebook logo automatically takes you to the web, where you can log in (see Figure 12–1).

Figure 12–1. *Logging in to Facebook on the Kindle Fire*

The Facebook screen is very similar to what you see on an Android smartphone browser. In fact, it opens a bookmark to m.facebook.com, the mobile version of the site.

This is different than running Facebook on the official app for Android. For some reason, all the operations on Facebook for the Kindle Fire are not on the app. This could change in the future, but for now, Facebook on the Kindle Fire is only a web browser venture (see Figure 12–2).

Figure 12–2. *Facebook on the Kindle Fire*

Facebook on the Kindle Fire looks very different than what you normally see on a computer browser (see Figure 12–3).

Figure 12–3. *Facebook on a regular browser*

The postings look the same, but there isn't the space to see comments or Likes and Dislikes. If you want to view these features, tap them. If you want to go back to the site, tap Back, just like you would any web site.

Friend Requests, Messages, and Notifications haven't changed form, merely location.

Status

Tapping the Status button brings you to a screen like the one shown in Figure 12–4.

Figure 12–4. *Updating your Facebook status on the Kindle Fire*

You can post your current status. The plus sign designates "Who are you with?".

The "Where are you?" pushpin does not work on a Kindle Fire because it only works on Android phones that have a GPS chip installed. The Kindle Fire has no GPS capability, but you can enter your location manually.

The Share button is for filtering who can see your status update.

Photo

You can upload a photo provided it is on your Kindle device. You have the option of uploading from the Gallery, Quickoffice, or whatever photo-related app you have installed. Getting a photo onto your device involves either downloading it from the cloud as a document file, or through a wired connection with a USB cable. The process is almost exactly the same as uploading an image for an e-mail contact (see Chapter 11).

Check In

Facebook's check-in feature is a way to post your location, but this has to be done manually. For example, I live in Pullman, Washington. My city appears in a list of several locations with that name as soon as I start typing "Pullman".

Menu Bar

The menu bar includes access to Favorites, Apps, Lists, Account Settings, Privacy Settings, Help Center, and Log Out. Figure 12–5 shows what this looks like on my device.

Figure 12–5. *The Menu bar for Facebook on the Kindle Fire*

It is quite simple to update Facebook on the Kindle Fire. I leave it up to you if it is faster to post photos from your computer rather than the Kindle Fire. If you want to update your status and look at the status of others, the Kindle Fire is a good tool.

Another social network that is very good on the Kindle Fire is Twitter.

Twitter

There is a Twitter Mobile Web (Kindle Fire Edition) app at the Amazon Appstore (see Figure 12–6).

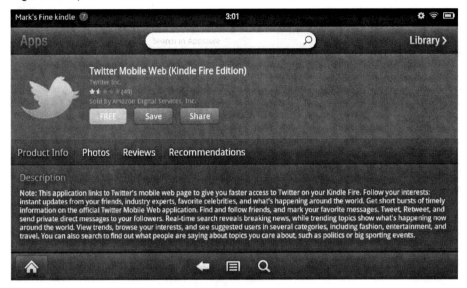

Figure 12–6. *Twitter Mobile Web for the Kindle Fire*

The Twitter program is very similar to the Facebook program; it reads off the web. You can sign up or sign in at the first screen, as shown in Figure 12–7.

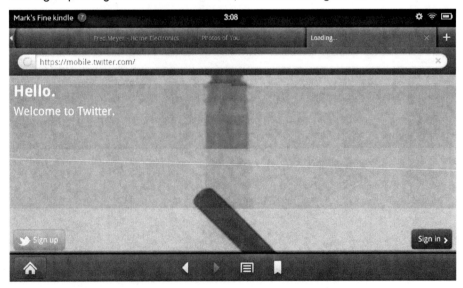

Figure 12–7. *Sign in to Twitter from the Kindle Fire*

Sign in with your Twitter username, not an e-mail address, as you do at a computer (see Figure 12–8).

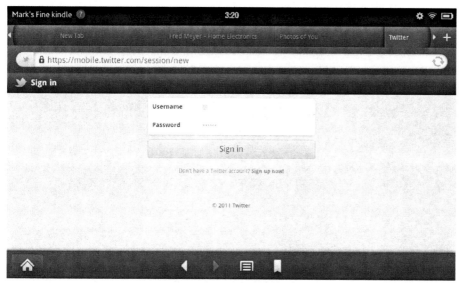

Figure 12–8. *Signing in on Twitter after the app has downloaded*

Open your Twitter account to find a list of options underneath the address bar (see Figure 12–9).

Figure 12–9. *See all tweets on the Kindle Fire*

The Twitter menu bar offers the following:

- *Home*: The screen that the Twitter app defaults to. It shows all recent tweets. If they are not recent enough, tap the Refresh button on the web site address bar.

- *Connect*: Allows you to attempt to connect with another Twitter subscriber. A search engine allows you to enter Interactions and Mentions (see Figure 12–10).

Figure 12–10. *The Collect option on Twitter for the Kindle Fire*

- *Discover*: Find the latest Twitter stories, trends, and who to follow; you can also browse categories (see Figure 12–11).

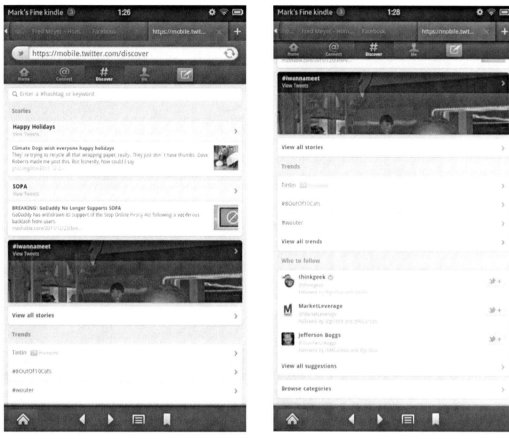

Figure 12–11. *Selecting Discover on Twitter for the Kindle Fire*

- *Me*: Displays your number of tweets, who is following you, and your number of followers. There are other options, as you can see in Figure 12–12.

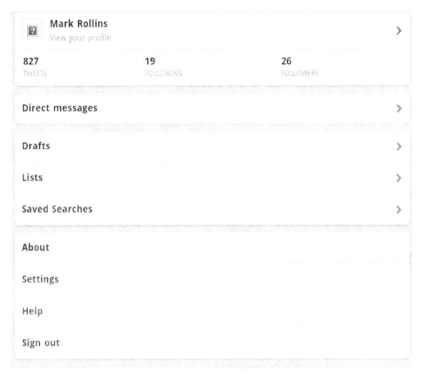

Figure 12–12. *Viewing your profile on Twitter for Kindle Fire*

▦   *Tweet*: The blue quill is there for you to enter your next tweet.

LinkedIn

LinkedIn is a popular business-related social networking site. Like Twitter, LinkedIn has an app; it can be accessed at the Amazon Appstore for Android. Unlike Twitter, all of the features on LinkedIn are available on the app.

Login with your e-mail and password (see Figure 12–13, left). If you don't have a LinkedIn account, go to the web site at www.linkedin.com. Once you are logged in, the app's home screen presents several options (see Figure 12–13, right).

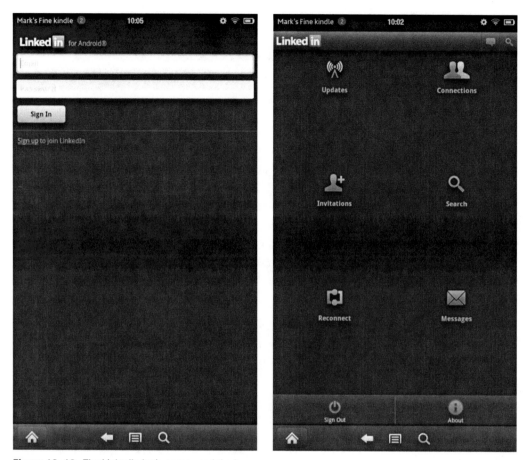

Figure 12–13. *The LinkedIn login screen and the home screen*

The following are LinkedIn's options available from its home screen:

- *Updates*: LinkedIn is all about the updates. It shows how one contact is connected to another, and so on. The blue dialogue balloon in the corner is for making your own update; the magnifying glass is the search engine; and the Home button returns you to the home screen (see Figure 12–14).

Figure 12–14. *The LinkedIn home screen*

■   *Connections*: Leads you to a list of your connections, the people who accept you as a connection. Connections appear alphabetically. Tapping the arrow beside each name provides e-mail message access (Figure 12–15).

Figure 12–15. *The Connections screen on the Kindle Fire*

- *Invitations*: Send or receive invites to the LinkedIn professional network. If you invite someone to join LinkedIn, then the message gives them instructions. If you have no pending invitations, the screen is blank. If you hit the Contents button, it allows you to Refresh.

- *Search*: If you are looking to connect to someone via LinkedIn, this is where you can perform a search for that person. You can also send an invite from here.

- *Reconnect*: Lists people that you might want to connect with. I believe that this information comes from people that you connect with in e-mail. There are also suggestions based on your workplace, university, and various other methods social networking uses to connect people.

- Messages: Check LinkedIn messages.

Google+

Google+ is a relatively new social networking site compared to Facebook, Twitter, and LinkedIn. It began in June 2011 as on a strictly "invitation only" basis. It is now open to anyone, without the need for an invite.

As of this writing, there is no Kindle Fire application available for Google+ or plain Google, for that matter. However, if you use the Kindle Fire's web browser to access a Gmail account, you see Google+ in the toolbar along with the Mail, Talk, and Calendar (see Figure 12–16).

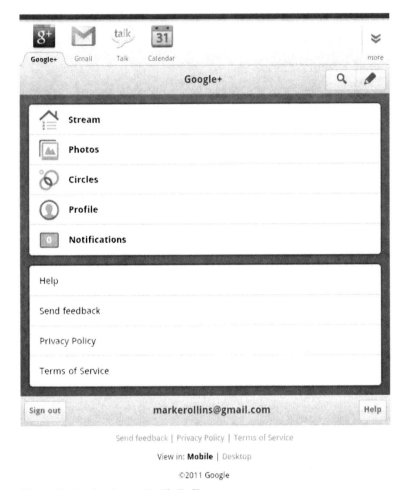

Figure 12–16. *Google+ on the Kindle Fire*

From here, you can update your status, as well as group your friends into circles.

Third-Party Social Media Apps

In addition to the social media apps that come with Kindle Fire, there are third-party apps that can make social networking on the Kindle Fire even better. I only discuss two apps, but I'm certain that there are and will be a whole lot more.

HootSuite

HootSuite is available at the Amazon Appstore for Android for free. It supports multiple social networks, like Twitter, Facebook, LinkedIn, and Foursquare, a social media site that provides "checking in" to certain places. It is very location-based. Foursquare does not have an official app for the Kindle Fire, but it is available on the iPhone and Android smartphones, as these have GPS capability.

Once HootSuite is downloaded, you set up your account through the login screen (see Figure 12–17, left). From there, enter an e-mail address and create a password (see Figure 12–17, right).

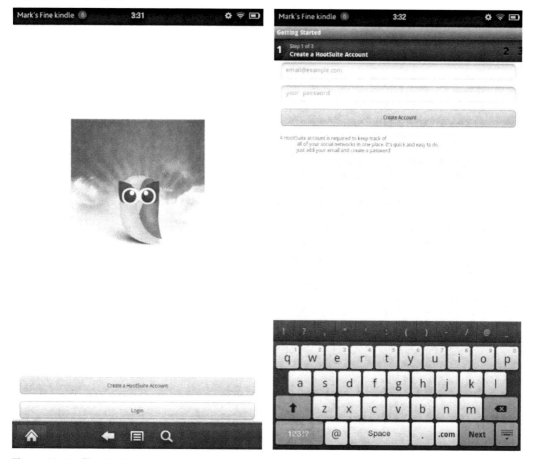

Figure 12–17. *The HootSuite home screen for the Kindle Fire (left), and creating a HootSuite account*

The next thing to do is connect to social networks. It is not necessary to connect to all four, but you have that option (see Figure 12–18).

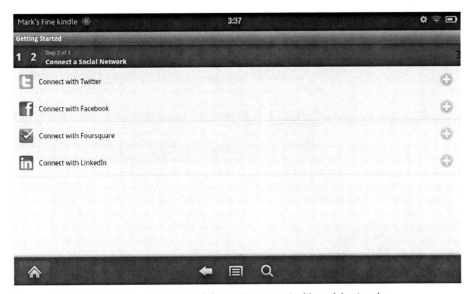

Figure 12–18. *HootSuite is set up so that it is easy to connect with social networks*

Tap the social media sites that you want to use on HootSuite and log in with your individual e-mails, phones, or whatever usernames are needed (see Figure 12–19, left). In some cases, you need to give permission to access your social media site (see Figure 12–19, right).

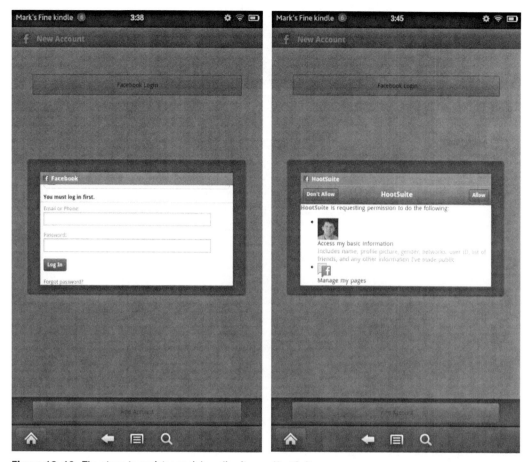

Figure 12–19. *The steps to register social media sites on HootSuite*

When you can check in at all your social networks, you get a screen that looks similar to Figure 12–20. When you are done adding social networks, tap the Done Adding Profiles button.

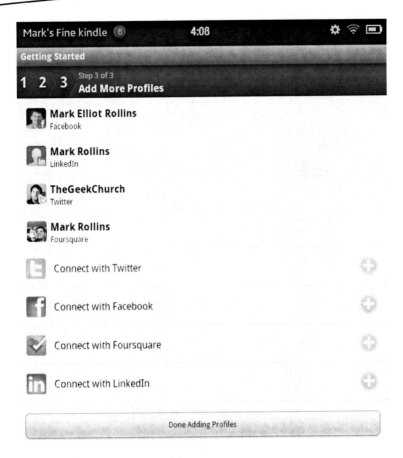

Figure 12–20. *Step 3 of the HootSuite setup*

You find all your social networks on one convenient page (see Figure 12–21, left). Each social network has two or more subjects. If you tap on the first one, you find that you can scroll vertically and horizontally. Notice the tiny dots located bottom center of each subject. These are the page designators; you can flip through your social network like pages on an e-book with left and right swipes (see Figure 12–21, right).

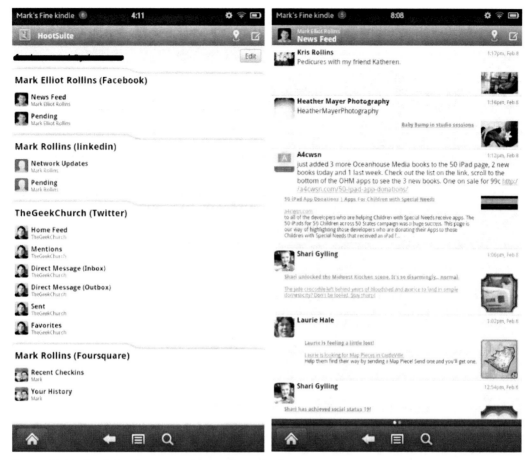

Figure 12–21. *HootSuite allows you to have social media sites on one page and flip through the sites like a book*

I would like to talk briefly about the symbols in the upper-right corner. The first is a pushpin, but honestly, this won't work for the present-day version of the Kindle Fire because it has no GPS capability. This may have improved since this writing; it would work well with Foursquare.

The pen and pad feature does different things depending on what social media site you are on. For Facebook and LinkedIn, it updates your status. For Twitter, it is how you tweet. For Foursquare, it is how you do a shout (see Figure 12–22).

To the left of the Send button are some interesting options. From left to right, they are as follows:

- *Photo*: If you have an image on the Kindle Fire, you can attach it here. Image files may be found in places like the Gallery or Quickoffice.

- *Calendar*: If you want to schedule a shout, tweet, or status, this opens a calendar so that you can select the exact time and date.

- *Shorten URLs*: Allows you to shorten URLs on an update, provided it can be abbreviated.

- *Location*: I cannot get this to work on my Kindle Fire. This is probably due to its lack of GPS functionality.

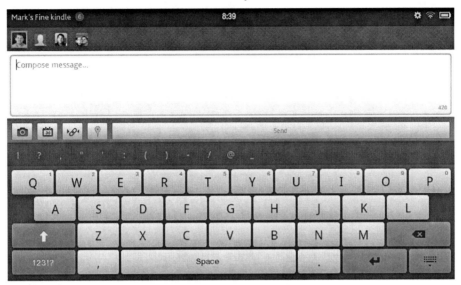

Figure 12–22. *Need to update your status? HootSuite allows you to do that*

Edit Streams provides two buttons (see Figure 12–23): Manage Tabs allows you to rename tabs and Social Networks allows you to add additional social networks.

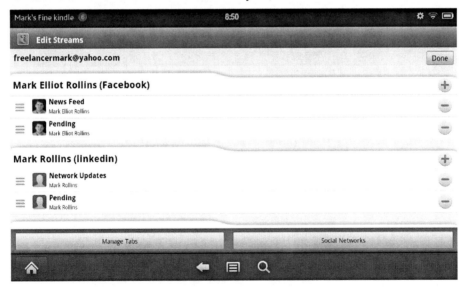

Figure 12–23. *The edit key is touched on HootSuite.*

The Contents menu has six categories (see Figure 12–24), which are as follows:

Figure 12–24. *The HootSuite Contents menu*

- *Search*: If you need to do a Twitter search, use this. As far as I can tell, it is not a search engine for the other social media sites.

- *Profiles*: Helpful for finding a person on Twitter.

- *Stats*: Examines the statistics and analytics for your Twitter identities.

- *Outbox*: View your outbox.

- *Places*: Takes you to the pushpin screen.

- *Settings*: Allows you to customize your social media experience.

TweetCaster

According to its web site, TweetCaster is the number-one Twitter app and has had millions of downloads. It has a lot of Twitter-related functions, such as "reading your timeline, viewing profiles, sending tweets, and clicking links". It has a version made just for the Kindle Fire (see in Figure 12–25, left) and is available for free on the Amazon Appstore for Android.

Log in and tap the plus sign in the corner. Sign in with your Twitter account (see Figure 12–25, right).

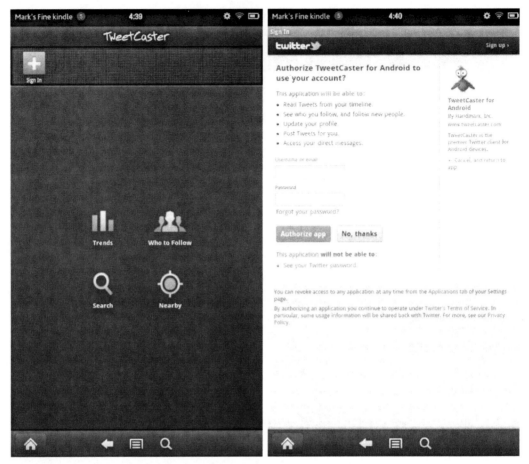

Figure 12–25. *The opening screen to TweetCaster (left) and the log in screen (right)*

Once you are signed in, you should see a screen similar to the one shown in Figure 12–26.

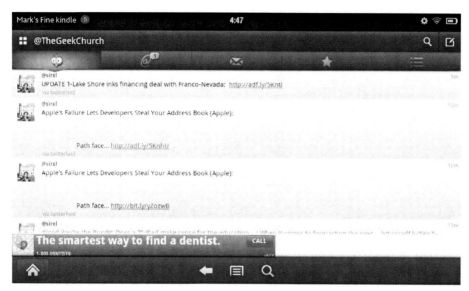

Figure 12–26. *The main page of TweetCaster*

There are five separate categories, as follows:

▨ *Tweets*: The people you tweet and the tweets of those that you follow are here.

▨ *Ampersand*: If you have been mentioned in a tweet, then it appears here with the @ before your Twitter username.

▨ *Messages*: Access your messages.

▨ *Favorites*: Access your favorites.

▨ *Lists*: Make a list on Twitter here.

Pressing and holding a tweet reveals a menu with all sorts of options (see Figure 12–27).

Figure 12–27. *The options for a tweet on TweetCaster*

Above the banner is a magnifying glass and a pad and paper; these are the search engine and tweet maker, respectively. The search engine is good for searching Twitter for all kinds of subjects (see Figure 12–28, left). The tweet maker is capable of reading a tweet (see Figure 12–28, right).

Figure 12–28. *The search engine for TweetCaster (left) and a tweet*

The Contents menu provides a variety of features, including the following:

- Jump to Top
- Refresh
- Settings
- Smart Filter
- People
- More, which includes additional categories, as follows:
  - Quick Follow
  - Find Friends
  - Twitter Status
  - Refresh All

- Exit Application

- About

Summary

The Kindle Fire may not be designed to be the ultimate social networking device, but it has the capability as long as it is connected to a Wi-Fi access point.

Facebook has an app for the Kindle Fire, but it opens in the web. From there, you can update your Facebook status, send messages to friends, upload photos, and even check in manually with your current location. Twitter is also enabled from the web; you can tweet and check out all the latest tweets.

The LinkedIn app allows you to check updates, connections, messages, and invitations. Another useful social network that is growing in popularity is Google+, which is easy to access with Gmail.

You should also check out the third-party apps designed to make social networking easier, like HootSuite and TweetCaster. HootSuite puts four major social networking sites in one place, making them easier and faster to manage.

Chapter 13

Quickoffice and Quickoffice Pro

What good is a tablet PC if one doesn't have a word processing program? According to the maker, "Quickoffice Pro is the first and only full-featured Microsoft Office productivity suite for Android devices with integrated access to multiple cloud storage providers."

I'm sure that most of us cannot live a day without accessing such programs as Word, Excel, PowerPoint, and Adobe Reader. Fortunately, Quickoffice provides limited mobile versions of these programs. Quickoffice Pro is set up so you can create, save, and edit documents.

The Kindle Fire is a Wi-Fi-only device. So, if you want to work on a Word document, an Excel spreadsheet, a PowerPoint presentation, or a PDF file while on the road, you have to save to the Kindle Fire in offline mode. You can always transport your Quickoffice to your home or work computer via wired connection.

Another option is to strategically plan your trip so that you can work on documents offline on Quickoffice, and then save them to the cloud. Cloud storage is networked and data is stored virtually by third-party hosting companies. Quickoffice is set up to work with hosting companies that provide more space to store your files. You need to set up a cloud storage service account, and possibly pay a fee, depending on the amount of cloud storage space that you want. Once your data is on the cloud, it can be accessed from many devices, including a network-connected laptop, desktop, or mobile phone.

Quickoffice

Fortunately, the Kindle Fire is set up with Quickoffice; it is on the Apps shelf ready to use. Unfortunately, the default version of Quickoffice is somewhat limited. If you want to upgrade to the full version, then you need to go to the Amazon Appstore and search for Quickoffice Pro (see Figure 13–1). I discuss the benefits of Quickoffice Pro later in this chapter, but for now, I want to talk about Quickoffice features.

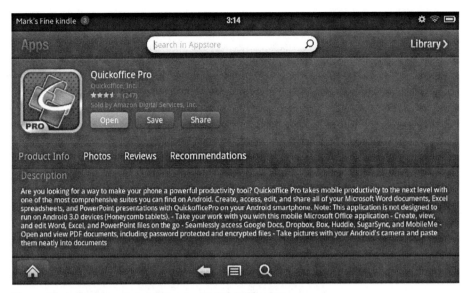

Figure 13–1. *The Amazon Appstore entry for Quickoffice Pro*

In either version of Quickoffice, you must first register. Registering allows you to stay current with the latest updates, features, and services available to you (see Figure 13–2).

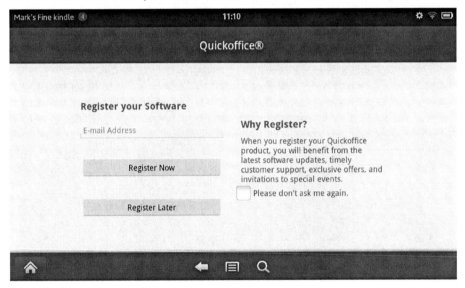

Figure 13–2. *Registering your Quickoffice software*

After registration, the Quickoffice opening screen should look like Figure 13–3.

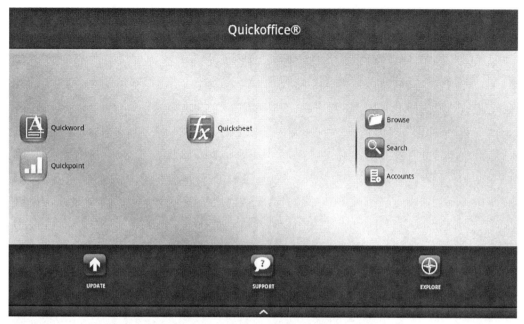

Figure 13–3. *The opening screen of Quickoffice, default version for the Kindle Fire*

Quickoffice Opening Menu Options

The default version of Quickoffice is really more of a viewer than a program to create and edit documents; however, it has features that work just as well as the Pro version.

On the home screen you find the following:

- *Quickword*: Handles Microsoft Word documents, such as .doc, .docx, .dot, .dotx, and .docm files.

- *Quicksheet*: Handles Microsoft Excel spreadsheet documents, such as .xls, .xlsx, and .xlsm files.

- *Quickpoint*: Handles Microsoft PowerPoint documents, such as .ppt, .pptx, .ppts, .pptm, and .pptsm files.

The other buttons on the screen are as follows:

- *Browse*: Allows you to look at your files (see Figure 13–4, left). Internal Storage opens a screen that shows all the folders on your Kindle Fire (see Figure 13–4, right); you should be able to find what you are looking for. Recent Documents shows which files were opened most recently.

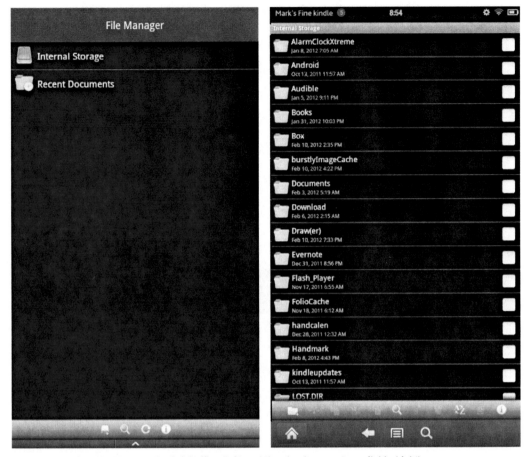

Figure 13–4. *The File Manager for Quickoffice (left) and the cloud accounts available (right)*

- *Search*: The search engine to locate files.

- *Accounts*: View all your documents on cloud hosting services (see Figure 13–5).

- *Update*: Updates Quickoffice Pro and Quickoffice.

- *Help*: Offers Quickoffice assistance; opens on the web.

- *Explore*: Opens a page to learn more about Quickoffice.

Documents on the Cloud

Once you open the Accounts file, you see a list of third-party cloud services for retrieving, storing, and editing documents (see Figure 13–5). Tapping any one of them allows you to set up an account.

Figure 13–5. *A list of some of the web-hosting cloud services that you can access from Quickoffice*

Google Docs

If you are new to cloud computing, most of the hosting companies on the Add Remote Account list may be unfamiliar to you. However, you probably have a Google account, and thus you already have 1 GB worth of cloud storage space on Google Docs.

If you haven't accessed Goggle Docs before, then open your Gmail account on your laptop or desktop. Click Documents on the top banner; this opens a screen similar to the one shown in Figure 13–6. I have several files in my Documents.

Figure 13–6. *Google Docs from my computer: all the files on the list are on the cloud*

If you are new to Google Docs, your list is blank. If you want to create documents on this extra gigabyte of space, click Create to begin a document, spreadsheet, presentation, form, drawing, table, or collection. The Upload button allows you to upload files from your computer to Google Docs. This button also allows you to purchase more cloud storage. At this writing, 20 GB of storage is $5 per year and 1 TB is $256 per year.

Let's say that you have uploaded all your files to Google Docs and you want to arrange it so that you can access your documents from Quickoffice. This is actually quite simple. Go to the Add Remote Account list and tap Google Docs. The first thing that you see is a quick warning window telling you that, "By using Google Docs, you understand that your files will be converted and some of your original formatting may be lost." If that bothers you, hit Cancel; otherwise, hit Continue.

You are then asked to enter your Gmail address and password (see Figure 13–7, left). Back at the home screen, tap Browse to see your list of documents, which includes Google Docs (see Figure 13–7, center). If you tap Google Docs, you should see all your documents (see Figure 13–7, right).

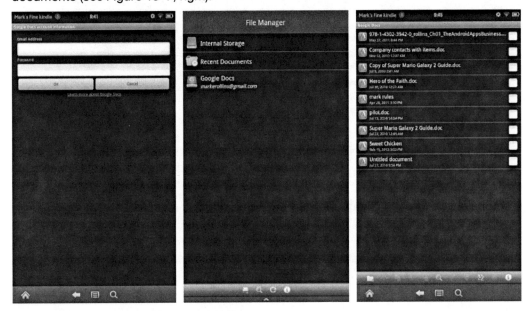

Figure 13–7. *Setting up Google Docs on Quickoffice*

Dropbox

Dropbox is another cloud service that you can use. Go to `www.dropbox.com` to download it to your desktop or laptop. It is very simple to set up, as you can see in Figure 13–8.

Figure 13–8. *Dropbox's web site offers easy-to-follow instructions for setting up on your computer*

One of Dropbox's best features is that it is on your computer's File Manager, so you can drag and drop files to it. It is a simple matter of copying and pasting a few files in Dropbox's Public folder. Dropbox also comes with a Photo folder.

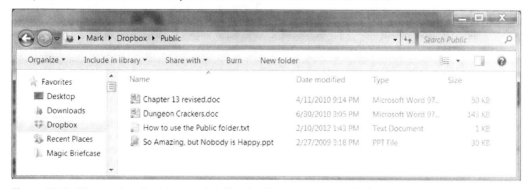

Figure 13–9. *It is easy to upload documents to Dropbox from your computer's file manager.*

Once you have your files in Dropbox, you can access the account on Quickoffice the same way as with Google Docs. Go to the home screen and select Dropbox. Enter your e-mail or username (see Figure 13–10).

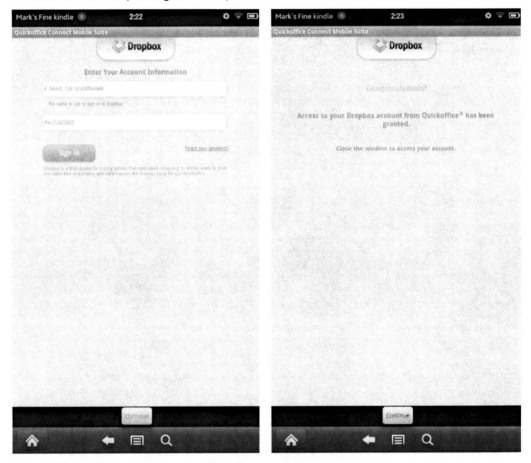

Figure 13–10. *Setting up Dropbox on your Kindle Fire*

Once you are set up on Dropbox, you can access files with the Browse button. Dropbox is also available from an iPhone or an Android phone.

Although Google Docs and Dropbox do not have official apps available for the Kindle Fire, programs such as SugarSync and Box do. They are set up in the same way as Google Docs and Dropbox.

With subscriptions to these cloud services, you should not have trouble finding space on the cloud to store a document. You can purchase more space at Google Docs and the other cloud services.

The Menu Bar on Quickoffice

The Quickoffice menu bar includes the following:

- *Disk Drive*: The icon that looks like a hard drive is designed to open an online account.

- *Search*: Locates files in the File Manager.

- *Upgrade*: The swirl icon might look like a "refresh" button, but it is all about getting upgrades for Quickoffice. It usually only upgrades to Quickoffice Pro.

- *Information*: Allows access to two areas: About shows the program's current version; Help opens the official Quickoffice for Android web site, where you can find answers and support (see Figure 13–11).

Figure 13–11. *The Help guide on Quickoffice*

Accessing a particular file on Quickoffice is done through the File manager, which has its own menu bar (see Figure 13–12).

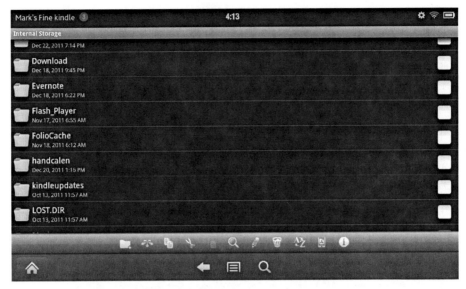

Figure 13–12. *The Internal Storage, with navigation bar*

You can do a lot with navigation bar, including the following:

- *Create New Folder*: Allows you to create a new folder for documents.

- *Send*: Sends a file as an attachment via e-mail.

- *Copy*: Copies a file to a clipboard, with the original document staying in its original location.

- *Cut*: Moves the folder to the clipboard.

- *Paste*: Places the previously cut or copied document to where you want it.

- *Search*: Locates a file.

- *Rename*: Allows you to change the name of a file, but I recommend keeping the suffix the same.

- *Delete*: Deletes a file completely.

- *Sort*: Organizes files by
  - Name
  - Type
  - Size
  - Date

- *Info*: Provides information on a file, including the file size.

- *Help*: Opens About and Help, as previously described.

Quickoffice Pro

I suggest updating to Quickoffice Pro, which lets you create and edit documents. Next, I describe its features.

Quickword

Quickword lets you view and edit Microsoft Word documents. It defaults a document to reflow view, which essentially places the text in such a way that scrolling left or right is not needed.

When you open the program, you have the option of creating a new document or opening on the SD card. The SD card section does not refer to an actual SD card, as this version of the Kindle Fire does not have a slot for memory expansion. The SD card does show what is on the Kindle Fire's current memory. Pressing New Document opens the list of choices shown in Figure 13–13.

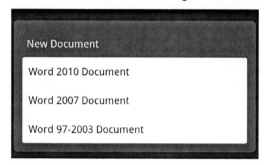

Figure 13–13. *Creating a new document on Quickword*

You have a lot of document options. When you tap the Content bar, a new menu bar opens, as you can see at the bottom of Figure 13–14.

Figure 13–14. *A new document on Quickword, with menu bar*

The following is a description of the menu bar buttons, from left to right:

- *File*: Features four different commands, as follows:

  - *Open*: Opens a document, which leads you back to the File Manager screen.

  - *New*: Opens a new document.

  - *Save*: Saves a document. You decide where to save it on the File Manager.

  - *Save As*: Saves a document with a different name or to a different file folder.

- *Font/Paragraph*: Changes the typeface or the layout of a page.

  - *Font*: Change the font type, the font size, and select boldface, italics, underline, and more (see Figure 13–15).

Figure 13–15. *The Font bar on Quickword*

  - *Paragraph*: Allows you to select line spacing and alignment, as well as bullets and other lists (see Figure 13–16).

Figure 13–16. *The Paragraph bar on Quickword*

- *Keyboard*: Brings the keyboard into view.

- *Search/Replace*: Helps the user search for a word or group of words in a document (see Figure 13–17).

Figure 13–17. *The Search/Replace bar on Quickword*

- *Image*: Place an image in your document. The image has to be from the Gallery. You might notice the option to Take Image with Camera, but since this version of the Kindle Fire doesn't have a camera, you won't get that one to work.

- *Undo*: Take back the last action you performed in the document.

- *Redo*: Reverses the Undo action.

- *Page View*: Makes a page easier to read by focusing on the text instead of the page.

- *Speech-to-Text*: Reads aloud the text on the page. This is done in a rather robotic voice, but if you are driving on a long road trip and want to hear something along the way, this is your tool!

- *Info*: Features the following:

  - *Properties*: Tells you information about your document, such as the file name and the size.

  - *Updates*: Checks for up-to-date firmware for Quickoffice.

  - *About*: Gives information about the Quickoffice software.

  - *Help*: Goes straight to the help screen on the office Quickoffice for Android web site.

Quicksheet

Quicksheet allows you to create and/or edit Excel documents, complete with rows, columns, spaces, and tabs. Unfortunately, not all Excel features are supported. A menu bar appears when you tap the Contents button (see Figure 13–18).

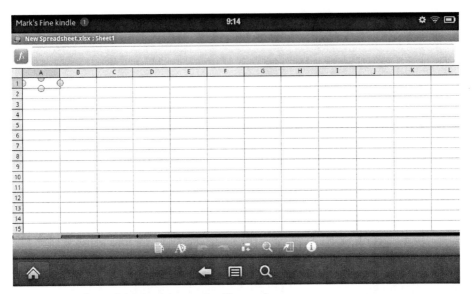

Figure 13–18. *A new Quicksheet document, with menu bar*

The following describes the buttons on the menu bar, from left to right:

- *File*: Features four commands, the same as in Quickword: Open, New, Save, and Save As.

- *Layout*: Acts similar to the Layout button in Quickword.

  - *Font*: Allows for changing the font, the font size, and boldface/italics/underline, and more (see Figure 13–19).

Figure 13–19. *The Font bar on Quicksheet*

  - *Alignment*: Adjusts the alignment (see Figure 13–20).

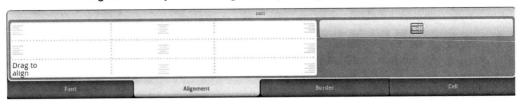

Figure 13–20. *The Alignment bar on Quicksheet*

  - *Border*: Adjusts the border around a cell or rows or columns (see Figure 13–21).

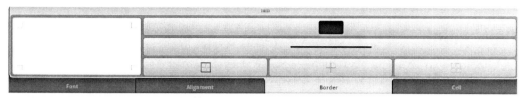

Figure 13–21. *The Border bar on Quicksheet*

> ▩ *Cell*: Offers everything else that you need to adjust a cell (see Figure 13–22).

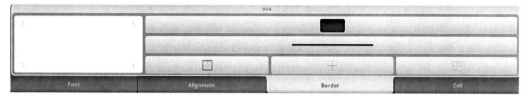

Figure 13–22. *The Cell bar on Quicksheet*

- ▩ *Undo*: In case you perform an action on your document that you want to take back, this is the button to push, just like on Quickword.

- ▩ *Redo*: This is also just like Quickword. In case you discovered that you actually want to do the action that you just hit Undo for, this button brings it back.

- ▩ *Format*: Insert or delete rows or columns.

- ▩ *Search/Replace*: Searches the document for words and/or phrases and possibly replacing them with other words and/or phrases.

- ▩ *Enter Cell Address*: Anytime that you want to find a certain cell, just enter the proper row and column number here to find it.

- ▩ *Info*: Features the following:

  - ▩ *Properties*: Shows information about your document, such as the file name and the size.

  - ▩ *Updates*: Checks for up-to-date firmware for Quick Office.

  - ▩ *About*: Gives you the information about the Quickoffice software.

  - ▩ *Help*: Goes straight to the help screen on the Quickoffice for Android web site.

Quickpoint

Quickpoint is an excellent way to create and edit PowerPoint documents on the Kindle Fire. An example is shown in Figure 13–23.

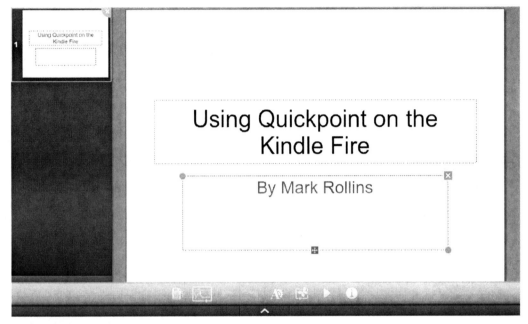

Figure 13–23. *A new document on Quickpoint*

The Contents menu is similar to Quickword and Quicksheet, as follows:

- *File*: Offers New, Open, Save, and Save As.
- *Tools*: Allows you to alter the current slide with text and shapes. It includes
  - Text Box
  - Rectangle
  - Rounded Rectangle
  - Oval
  - Line
  - Left Arrow
  - Right Arrow
  - Up Arrow
  - Down Arrow

- *Undo*: In case you perform an action on your document that you want to take back, this is the button to push, just like on Quickword.

- *Redo*: This is also just like Quickword. In case you discovered that you actually want to do the action that you just hit Undo for, this button brings it back.

- *Layout*: Alters text and more. It includes

    - *Font*: Alters the typeface in a document (see Figure 13–24).

Figure 13–24. *The Font bar on Quickpoint*

    - *Paragraph*: Adjusts the alignment of the text in the text box (see Figure 13–25).

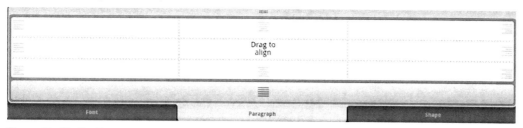

Figure 13–25. *The Paragraph bar on Quickpoint*

    - *Shape*: Adds color to the text or border (see Figure 13–26).

Figure 13–26. *The Shape bar on Quickpoint*

- *Image*: Just like on Quickword, this is how to insert an image onto Quickpoint, provided it is taken from the Gallery.

- *Slideshow*: Begins the slideshow. If you can mount your Kindle Fire on a stand, you have what you need to make a presentation!

- *Info*: Features Properties, Updates, About, and Help.

QuickPDF

QuickPDF provides a quick way to view PDF files. There are many options when you hit the Contents menu (see Figure 13–27).

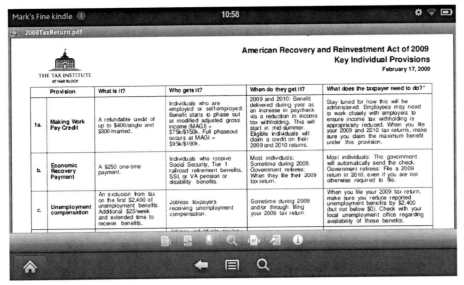

Figure 13–27. *A new file on QuickPDF*

The buttons on the menu bar are as follows:

- *File*: The only thing that you can do here is open a file.

- *Page View*: View the page as text or in full view.

- *Bookmark*: Access any bookmarks.

- *Search*: Searches and highlights the document for specific words or phrases (see Figure 13–28).

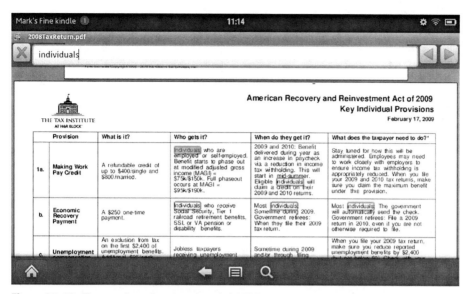

Figure 13–28. *The search engine at work on QuickPDF*

- *Rotate*: Rotates the document left or right 90 degrees in either direction.

- *Page Number*: Jump to a particular page by entering the page number.

- *Info*: The usual features—Properties, Updates, About and Help.

Summary

The Kindle Fire comes with Quickoffice, a handy program for viewing Word, Excel, and PowerPoint documents. Users also have the ability to access files on cloud services like Google Docs, Dropbox, Huddle, and SugarSync. Storing your documents on these cloud services provides access to them from your computer or Android phone.

If you are looking for a way to do more with Quickoffice, I recommend upgrading to Quickoffice Pro. It costs more than most applications, but it really offers the best way to create and edit documents on the Kindle Fire. It also comes with QuickPDF for viewing Adobe files.

In short, Quickoffice turns the Kindle Fire into a mobile electronic office.

Chapter 14

Fun and Productive Apps for the Kindle Fire

One of the criticisms of Amazon's Kindle Fire is that it requires Wi-Fi to do any work that is accessible on the Cloud. Assuming that you have access to Wi-Fi, you can really do quite a lot on the Kindle Fire.

In fact, the Kindle Fire is set up to help you even if you are not online. In this last chapter, I discuss apps that help you become more productive or keep you entertained.

One habit that you want to develop is Wi-Fi porting, which is when you plan trips around places with free Wi-Fi hot spots, like libraries and coffee shops. This way, you can enjoy the fun and productive apps that make your Kindle Fire a more pleasant experience.

Calendars

The Kindle Fire is about the same size as a date planner or an appointment book. It is very easy to use the Kindle Fire as an appointment planner—and forget the day planner/appointment book altogether. Sadly, there isn't a default app included on the Kindle that acts as a calendar, like on most mobile phones.

The Hand Calendar App

A quick search on the Amazon Appstore for Android reveals several calendar apps that work well. For example, *Hand Calendar* is, as of this writing, the number-one calendar app (see Figure 14–1, left). *Hand Calendar* allows the user to mark certain dates by hand (see Figure 14–1, right). You can also use it to write a casual note, such as a grocery list. You can even make checklists.

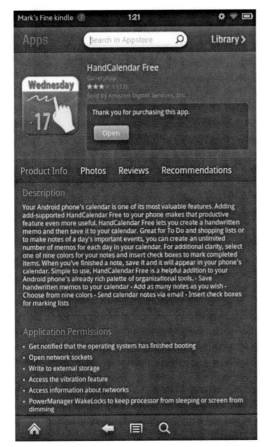 

Figure 14–1. *The Hand Calendar app for Kindle Fire*

The bad news about *Hand Calendar* is that although you can mark the month and day for an appointment, you cannot mark a specific hour unless you write in the time yourself. The good news is that you do not have to be connected to a Wi-Fi hot spot to use it.

If you are looking for more calendar-related apps, try "planner" or "scheduler" as a keyword search. You also might want to use a calendar application on the web, like Google Calendar.

Google Calendar

If you have constant access to Wi-Fi, then I recommend using Google Calendar. You need a Gmail account, but that is simple to set up, and you can access it very easily on the e-mail app.

Google Calendar provides access to any date to set up an appointment for any time (see Figure 14–2).

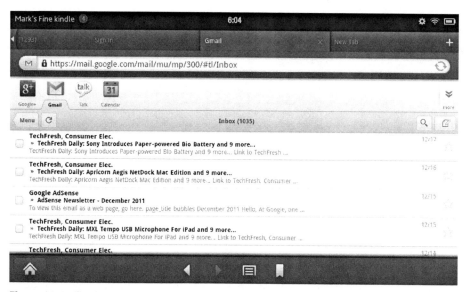

Figure 14–2. *The Gmail site, with the Calendar option on the top menu bar*

The problem with using Gmail on the Kindle Fire is that it requires that the user be online to use. The good news is that once an appointment is entered in the Google Calendar, it shows up anywhere you open it, from your computer to your smartphone. In other words, the appointment that you make is easily retrievable from wherever you can get the internet.

All that is required is to select the day, then hit the plus sign in the upper-right corner. Enter the appointment name in the What area. In the When area, enter the date and time. You can select the appointment time from start to end, in half-hour increments. From there, enter the location of the meeting in the Where section.

Under Calendar, you can select the Gmail account that you are using, in case you have more than one. The Description is a good place for notes on what needs to happen before or during the meeting (see Figure 14–3).

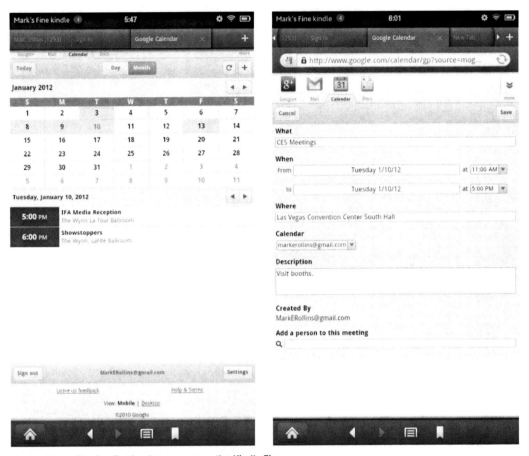

Figure 14–3. *The Gmail calendar, as seen on the Kindle Fire*

If you are looking for a calendar app that syncs with your Google Calendar, I suggest an app like *CalenGoo*, which costs $5.99 at the Amazon Appstore for Android (see Figure 14–4, left). I also suggest more advanced calendar apps such as *Pocket Informant*, which costs $12.99 (see Figure 14–4, right).

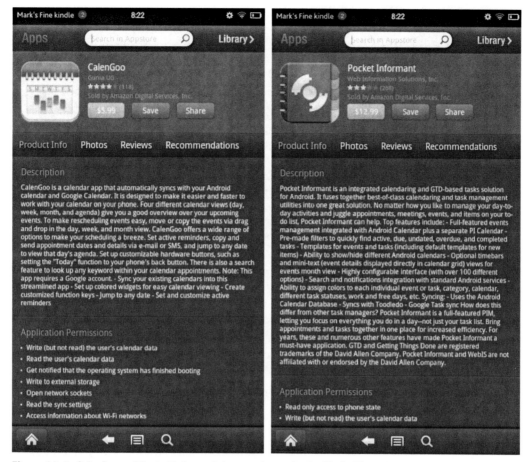

Figure 14–4. *CalenGoo and Pocket Informant, two great apps for the Kindle Fire to help sync your Google Calendar*

Alarm Clocks

Of course, if you have a calendar app, then you need an appointment alert. I suggest an alarm clock, assuming your planner or calendar app does not have a method to notify you of a new appointment.

Even though there is no app included on the Kindle Fire, running a search for alarm clock reveals many options. One of them is *Alarm Clock Xtreme*, which is available for free at the Kindle Fire Appstore (see Figure 14–5).

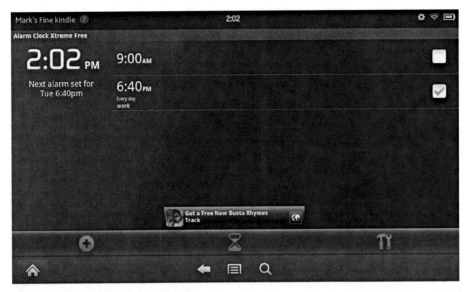

Figure 14–5. *The Alarm Clock Xtreme app*

Setting the alarm on *Alarm Clock Xtreme* is very simple. All that is required is to tap one of the already present times, and you are able to reset the alarm to a different time. You can program the time to repeat on different days of the week, or every day. You can also select a label so when an alarm tone goes off, you know why.

Yes, it does help to have an alarm app, and there is an added bonus on *Alarm Clock Extreme*—you can set a timer. So if you have to do something in a certain amount of time, it is easy to set up.

Drawing Programs

Sometimes you want the freedom to jot down a note, and maybe make a little drawing as well. For this reason, you want to download a program that allows you to draw on the Kindle Fire's touchscreen. You also might want to get a stylus. You definitely want to make certain that it is a conductive stylus, an accessory that I discussed in Chapter 3.

Drawing Pad

One of the top programs is the *Drawing Pad*, which is available for $1.99. It provides options for some incredible pictures (see Figure 14–6).

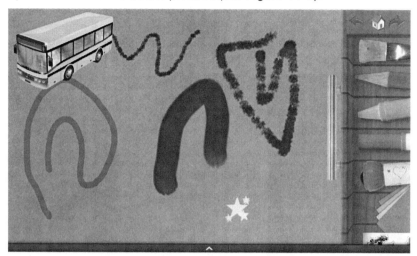

Figure 14–6. *The Drawing Pad app for the Kindle Fire*

The brush, colored pencil, crayon, marker, and stamp are the tools that you can use to draw. You can change the color and type of paper, and add stickers like that bus shown in the corner of Figure 14–6. It is like having an art studio on your Kindle Fire. You can share your work with any app that accepts a picture. You can also save the picture to your Gallery.

SketchBook Mobile

Another great drawing program available for the Kindle Fire is *SketchBook Mobile*, by Autodesk Inc. (see Figure 14–7, left). It has a similar system of artistic tools, but the interface is slightly different than that of *Drawing Pad*. In *SketchBook Mobile*, the user presses a button to open a circular menu with pencils, text, eraser, and other drawing tools (see Figure 14–7, right). *SketchBook Mobile* is available for $1.99 on the Amazon Appstore for Android. You can also get a free version, *SketchBook Mobile Express*.

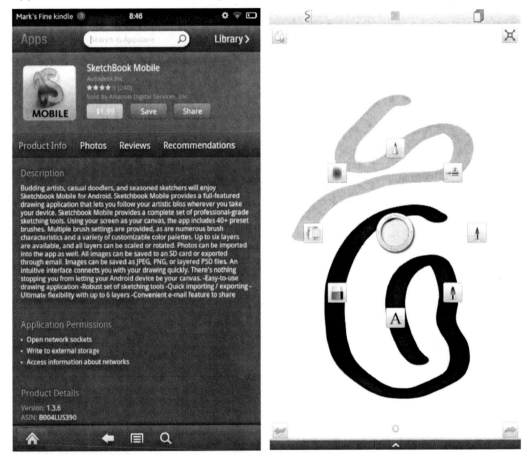

Figure 14–7. *The SketchBook Mobile app as it appears on the Amazon Appstore for Android (left), and how it actually runs (right)*

iSketch

If you are looking for something that is just a pad and paper, *iSketch* seems to do the job (see Figure 14–8).

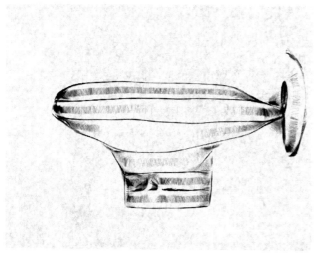

Figure 14–8. *A sample illustration for iSketch on the Kindle Fire*

As you can see in Figure 14–8, *iSketch* files tend to have a very pencil-and-paper look to them. I tried to draw some sort of flying machine like a blimp, as *iSketch* reminds me of the sketches of Leonardo da Vinci and his unusual flying machines. Even though my sketch is in black and white, it is possible to change the pen's color.

The trick to drawing on *iSketch* is to draw fast for thin lines and slow for thick lines. It is also possible to change the textures. You can save pictures to the Gallery.

Flashlights

You never know when you might find yourself stumbling around in the dark in need of a light. There are many apps that can be used as a flashlight on the Kindle Fire. I suggest a very useful app known as *Color Flashlight*. It essentially turns the Kindle Fire screen into a bright light, which I can't really show in a screenshot. *Color Flashlight* is available on the market if you want to see its features (see Figure 14–9).

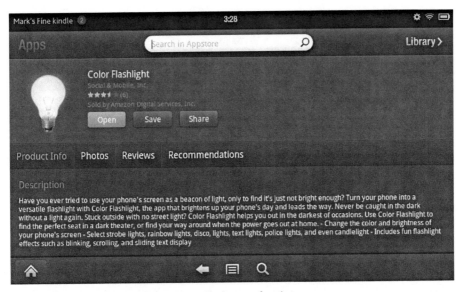

Figure 14–9. *The Color Flashlight entry on the Amazon Appstore*

Not only is this a good app for providing light, but it has bonus features like making cool illuminated patterns and creating a handheld neon sign.

Calculators

In all honesty, I would have included a calculator with the default apps; but then, I am not Amazon. Honestly, our first pocket mobile devices were calculators, and I consider a device like a cellular phone incomplete if it doesn't have some way to make calculations. After all, who doesn't need to make a simple or complex calculation every now and then?

I recommend doing a search on "calculator" in Apps. You will find plenty. I found one called *Office Calculator* (see Figure 14–10, left). It is more than just a calculator. It can look like a regular calculator, or perhaps an adding machine (see Figure 14–10, right), complete with white tape.

Figure 14–10. *The Office Calculator entry on the store, and the app at work*

There are other calculator apps available for the Kindle Fire. A notable one is the *Scientific Graphing Calculator*, useful for math students (see Figure 14–11).

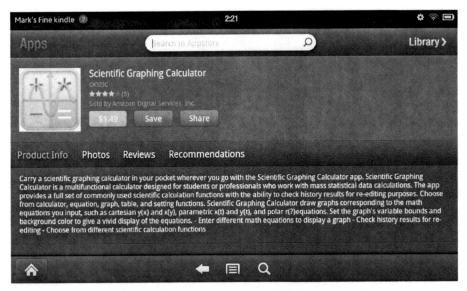

Figure 14–11. *The Scientific Graphing Calculator for the Kindle Fire*

Notepads

If you don't want to spend the money on Quickoffice Pro to take notes, then I recommend downloading a free notepad app like *Notepad* (see Figure 14–12). It is good for creating a note, saving it, and deleting it when you no longer need it.

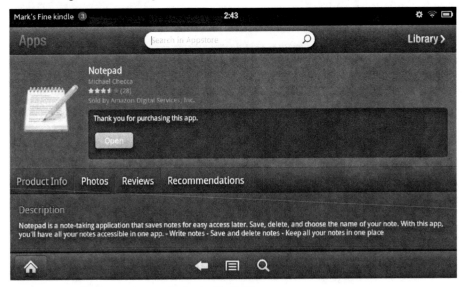

Figure 14–12. *The Notepad app entry for the Kindle Fire*

Evernote

If you want to do more complicated note taking and make it so you can access your notes online, then you should go with *Evernote*. You can find it at the Kindle Fire Appstore. Hit the Create account on the login screen (see Figure 14–13); you are asked to enter a username and password.

Figure 14–13. *The opening screen for Evernote*

Evernote works a lot like the Gmail Calendar—any note can essentially sync online to be accessed from one's mobile phone or computer. You can also use these devices to take notes. All your notes are visible whenever you open Evernote on whatever device (see Figure 14–14).

Figure 14–14. *Evernote on the Kindle Fire*

It is easy to create a new note, but the Kindle Fire does not allow for adding audio or a camera picture. The picture of the downloaded photo in Figure 14–14 comes from an *Evernote* note that I created on my computer. By the way, you can also use *Evernote* notes on Quickoffice Pro, which allows you to access *Evernote* from cloud accounts (see Chapter 13). *Evernote* is one of the best ways to put your thoughts on your Kindle Fire.

Games

I think we all know that even though we probably shouldn't, we all play games. Sure, we could use all the productive apps on the Kindle Fire to make our lives smoother, but sometimes, we just get bored with our work and want to have a little bit of fun. For this reason, there are many applications for the Kindle Fire that are games. You will find that many of these games are a very pleasant way to pass the time, and they are also extremely addictive.

Angry Birds

It is very difficult to talk about any successful gaming app without mentioning Rovio's monster mobile game, *Angry Birds*. Millions are addicted to this game, which has a very simple premise. The user shoots birds with a slingshot (using a finger swipe), and knocks over fragile structures in order to kill a bunch of greedy pigs. It is optimized for the Kindle Fire. It is better to play on a larger screen than a smaller one (see Figure 14–15).

Figure 14–15. *Oh, the fun of Angry Birds, a game worth downloading, sometimes for free.*

If this is not enough, you can also download *Angry Birds Seasons*, or a version based on the movie *Rio*. You can usually get these for free; an ad-free version has a price.

Fruit Ninja

Another very addictive game that requires nothing more than a finger to play is *Fruit Ninja* (see Figure 14–16). The game is very simple in its premise: as fruit flies into the air, you must cut it before it falls. Of course, you also have bombs, which you don't want to chop, constantly get in the way.

Figure 14–16. *Graphics from Fruit Ninja*

Once again, this is a game that has different versions (some with a price tag). One version is based on the Dreamworks movie *Puss in Boots*.

Paper Toss

Paper Toss is a game that has very few complications. Chuck a wadded up piece of paper into a garbage can via finger swipes on the touchscreen. You probably do this in reality when you are bored at the office; the only difference is that you probably don't have a fan that blows off your aim (see Figure 14–17).

Figure 14–17. *The main menu and gameplay for Paper Toss*

Where's My Water?

Where's My Water is a game from Disney Interactive (see Figure 14–18, left). It has become one of the most addictive games since *Angry Birds*. The premise is somewhat complex. There is an alligator named Swampy who is trying to take a bath. There is water available, but it has to flow to get to Swampy's drainpipe. The object is to use a finger or stylus to "dig" through the dirt and get the water to flow to Swampy while removing three rubber ducks along the way to maximize on score (see Figure 14–18, right). There are also time bonuses per level. You can even find hidden objects while digging through the dirt. Finding all the hidden objects can lead to bonus levels.

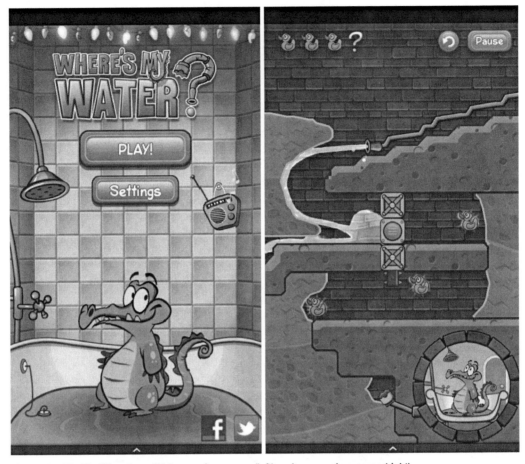

Figure 14–18. *The Where's my Water opening screen (left) and a gameplay screen (right)*

Words with Friends

If you ever played *Scrabble*, then you know how to play *Words with Friends*. You need to set up an account on Facebook or use an e-mail address to play against an opponent on a virtual game board (see 14–19, left). In Figure 14–19 (right), note the TW, DL, DW, TL; this where you can make some extra points with triple word, double letter, double word, and triple letter, respectively. This game is available by default on the Kindle Fire Apps Library, but you need to install it (see Chapter 9).

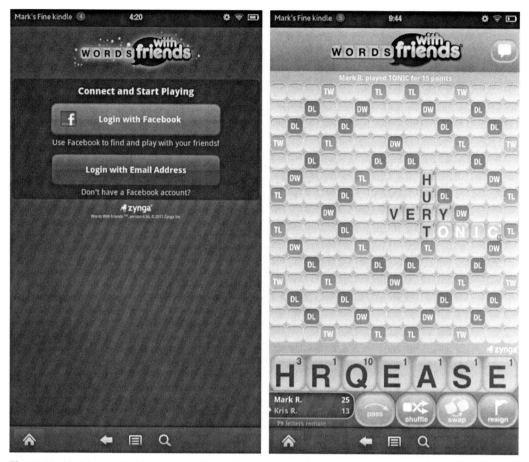

Figure 14–19. *Words with Friends, a Scrabble-like game made for mobile devices and available on the Kindle Fire*

Summary

The Kindle Fire comes with a lot of terrific programs, but some helpful ones are missing. Fortunately, it is easy to download the programs that you need.

You can download several calendar programs for setting appointments, or you can use the Google Calendar when you are online. The same goes for *Notepad*, which has offline apps, or online programs like *Evernote*.

Apps such as alarm clocks, drawing programs, calculators, and flashlights are helpful. There are also some pretty incredible games like *Angry Birds*, *Fruit Ninja*, *Paper Toss*, *Where's My Water*, *Words with Friends*, and much more.

Of course, these are not the only apps that will make your Kindle Fire a productive tool. In the few months that I have had mine, I found that I was able to simply do more with a portable device than I could on a desktop or even a laptop.

In a way, unlocking a Kindle Fire is a lot like opening the door to your home after a long day at work. You can relax as you read a magazine or book, listen to music, or watch a video. You can also have fun on the web or with various apps. The Kindle Fire can also be a work place because you can do work using Quickoffice and anything else from the Docs category.

The Kindle Fire is something that helps me do more work and play more. I hope that this book has shown you how to do more of both as well.

At this writing, the Kindle Fire is a super-hit product that has sold in the millions. I have little doubt that Amazon will create an upgrade to the Kindle Fire. Perhaps they will follow Apple's current business model for the iPad and release a new version every year. If they do, I look forward to a Kindle Fire with Bluetooth, an optional keyboard, an HDMI port, and other advancements. However, if the Kindle Fire never has any upgrades, it really is more than enough, especially with its Cloud.

So enjoy working and playing on the Kindle Fire as much as I have. There's an old saying, "You only get out of it what you put into it." In other words, if you want something or somebody to give you something, then you have to be willing to give for it. In the same way, invest a lot of time in the Kindle Fire, and what you get will be so much more.

Index

CPSIA information can be obtained at www.ICGtesting.com
Printed in the USA
LVOW130718250412

279042LV00012B/1/P